Harvey Lee Ross

The Early Pioneers and Pioneer Events of the State of Illinois

Harvey Lee Ross

The Early Pioneers and Pioneer Events of the State of Illinois

ISBN/EAN: 9783337013578

Printed in Europe, USA, Canada, Australia, Japan

Cover: Foto ©ninafisch / pixelio.de

More available books at **www.hansebooks.com**

Harvey Lee Ross

THE
EARLY PIONEERS

AND

PIONEER EVENTS

OF THE STATE OF ILLINOIS

INCLUDING PERSONAL RECOLLECTIONS OF THE WRITER;
OF ABRAHAM LINCOLN, ANDREW JACKSON, AND
PETER CARTWRIGHT, TOGETHER WITH

A BRIEF AUTOBIOGRAPHY
OF THE WRITER.

BY HARVEY LEE ROSS

CHICAGO
EASTMAN BROTHERS
1899

DEDICATION.

To the few surviving companions and friends of the times and scenes of which I have written, and who shared with me the trials and triumphs of those long past pioneer years, this book is respectfully dedicated.

HARVEY L. ROSS.

PREFACE.

The author of this book being now a citizen of the City of Oakland, State of California, and in the eighty-first year of his age, having been an early pioneer of the State of Illinois, having settled there with his parents in the year 1820, and having lived to witness the rise and progress and the development of that great State from its infancy, and having been familiar with many circumstances and events connected with the early history of that State, and having been well acquainted with Abraham Lincoln and Peter Cartwright from their first coming into the State up to the time of their respective deaths, and having also had the privilege and the opportunity of learning much about the early life and adventures of Andrew Jackson, was solicited by friends who had been informed of these facts to write for publication what he knew concerning pioneer times and those illustrious men.

In compliance to such requests he wrote a number of articles which were published in the Fulton Democrat at Lewistown, Fulton County, Illinois, and which were copied into other newspapers, and since such publication he has been further solicited by many persons to have those articles compiled and published in book form, and they now here appear substantially as they were copied from those papers.

HARVEY LEE ROSS.

OAKLAND, CALIFORNIA, 1898.

NOTE.—A few months ago, while on a business trip to San Francisco, California, I visited my uncle at his home near by Oakland, and was there shown many of the communications here appearing. The writer of this memorandum note was deeply impressed with the future value of these writings as representing an accurate and faithful narration of events of the early days of the now great State of Illinois, and as being replete with interesting remembrances and unrecorded sayings and doings of three now historical characters.

I urged upon my uncle the privilege and duty even that rested with and upon him, to put his newspaper and fugitive writings into final form for book publication, so that they could pass into the permanent literature of the State and not perish. It was easily seen that the terse and ofttimes quaint statements of facts and events had a peculiar attractiveness of expression of their own, and the honesty and candor that permeate every line of his writings doubly assure a recognition of value.

I found my uncle, although past the four-score years of the psalmist, hale in body, bright and cheerful, and in as full possession of his mental strength and vigor as in the noontime of his life. Indeed, you could say of him as Sir Walter Scott has so beautifully spoken of one of his characters of fiction, "that the snows of Winter have fallen upon, but chilled him not." I found to my gratification that my uncle had also thought of preserving his writings in book form, at least for his descendants and friends, and he then gave me permission immediately so to do. I have taken the liberty of adding a reproduction of his portrait as a frontispiece, taken in the 80th year of his age.

CHARLES K. OFFIELD.

379 Ashland Boulevard, Chicago, Illinois.

December, 1898.

CONTENTS.

PIONEER TIMES.

CHAPTER I 1–5
    Pioneer journey from New York to Illinois.—The pirogue of the early settler.—Dr. Davison, the "Hermit," the first settler.

CHAPTER II 6–9
    The first murder among early pioneers.—The first lawyers.—Some errors in Chapman's History of Fulton County.

CHAPTER III 9–13
    Tragical death of Peter White.—The Ross ferry.—A fight between pioneers and Indians.

CHAPTER IV 14–17
    The ending of the Indian fight.—My boyhood ghost for an Indian scare.—My father's trade with the Indians.—Early religious customs of the Indians.—A war dance.

CHAPTER V 18–21
    An early pioneer dance.—Major Newton Walker and his fiddle.—A pioneer wagon ride.

CHAPTER VI 21–25
    The first log houses, their construction.—Old-fashioned fireplace; the latch-string; the hominy mortar; the reap-hook and flail.—The first horse-mill of the early settler.—"Squaw corn."—My mother's rescue of her kettle from the Indians, with her fire-shovel.

CHAPTER VII 26–30
    The Nimans.—First blacksmith shop opened by Jacob Niman.—Dr. Charles Newton, a celebrated pioneer physician.—Another error in Chapman's History.

CHAPTER VIII 30–34
    Pike County organized.—First election in Fulton County held at my father's house.—My father's vote the first cast in Fulton County.—John L. Bogardus, one of Peoria's early settlers.—First marriages in Fulton County.—My sister Lucinda the first white child born in this territory.

CHAPTER IX 35–38
    The Wentworths and early Chicago.—The Kingstons.—Brother Lewis' visit to Chicago.

CONTENTS.

CHAPTER X.. 38-41
The Havana Hotel; its construction.—Court held in bar-room of my hotel, where Abraham Lincoln attended.—Blockhouses built.

CHAPTER XI.. 41-45
Arrival of Judge Phelps and William Proctor.—Their kindness to the Indians.—Judge Phelps' sportsmanship.

CHAPTER XII... 45-50
How the fourteen pigeons were killed with a rifle-ball at one shot.—The first pioneer stores.—Method of shipping cargo to St. Louis.—The first penitentiary in the state.—Christian character and benevolent deeds of Myron Phelps and William Proctor.

CHAPTER XIII.. 50-55
The big snow of 1830-31 and terrible suffering therefrom.—Description of Indian wigwam.—Chief Raccoon and my "good luck."

CHAPTER XIV... 55-58
Meeting of brother Lewis and Chief Raccoon in Indian Reservation.—Indian traits.—Tragedy in Dean's Settlement.

CHAPTER XV.. 58-62
Captain John and his squaws.—The Indians' Paradise.—Indian traffic in ginseng and wild potatoes, and their extermination by wild hogs.

CHAPTER XVI... 62-66
Appearance of the country when early settlers arrived.—Extensive and beautiful prairies.—My experience in hauling hay.—Discovery of coal by Mr. Gardiner.—First banking establishment in Fulton County.

CHAPTER XVII.. 66-70
John Coleman, a remarkable pioneer.—Little Pike's first ride.

CHAPTER XVIII... 71-74
The Westerfield Indian scare.—Memorable cyclone of 1835.—Uprising of Canton's women against the saloons of that village.

CHAPTER XIX... 75-78
Pioneer hangings.—Early lawyers.

CHAPTER XX.. 78-81
Suicide of Edward Stapleford and its awful consequence.

CHAPTER XXI... 81-85
The pioneer doctor and his methods of treatment.—The Indian doctor.—How he cured me.

CONTENTS.   ix

CHAPTER XXII... 85-88
Pioneer schools.—First steel pens.—How some young ladies were punished for disobeying rules.—First schoolhouse and its construction.

CHAPTER XXIII.. 89-92
Letter from Mr. John W. Proctor.—My reply thereto.

ABRAHAM LINCOLN.

CHAPTER I... 93-95
Conditions under which I first became acquainted with Abraham Lincoln.

CHAPTER II.. 95-98
Lincoln the grocery clerk.—How he qualified himself for surveyor.

CHAPTER III... 98-101
Some errors in Herndon's "Life of Lincoln."—Anne Rutledge, Lincoln's first sweetheart, and her untimely death.

CHAPTER IV... 102-109
Lincoln's second sweetheart, Mary Owens.—His letter in regard to the breaking of the engagement.—First circus of pioneer days.

CHAPTER V.. 110-113
Lincoln's trip on a flatboat to New Orleans.—His visit to a slave market, and his avowed hatred and intention regarding the institution of slavery.

CHAPTER VI... 113-116
The first step to the White House.—The "shirt-sleeve court in the corn field."—Mr. Lincoln's refusal of a well-earned fee.

CHAPTER VII.. 116-120
How Lincoln first earned the sobriquet of "Honest Abe."—His speech wins the debate.—Circumstances of his speech in 1858 when running for senator.

CHAPTER VIII... 120-122
Some facts in relation to Lincoln's storekeeping.—Error in Herndon's biography.—Mr. Lincoln a judge in horse-races.

CHAPTER IX... 123-127
Some incidents of W. H. Herndon's early life.—His further misstatements in regard to Lincoln.

CONTENTS.

CHAPTER X..127-130
True story of the Lincoln-Shields duel.

CHAPTER XI...130-133
Mr. Lincoln's religious belief.

CHAPTER XII..134-136
My visit to the grave of the martyred president.

ANDREW JACKSON.

CHAPTER I..137-152
The Churchwell and Kirkpatrick families' personal acquaintanceship with the old hero and statesman.—History of the tragedy in which Andrew Jackson participated.—Our visit to him at the Hermitage.—Story of Mrs. Jackson's death.—A little anecdote about Alexander Kirkpatrick.

CHAPTER II...152-166
Brief history of Presidential election of 1828.—Some further incidents concerning Jackson.—Our delightful visit to the South.—How my son Frank finally came to partake of southern hospitality at the hands of "Aunt Moody."—Death of Andrew Jackson shortly after our return from the South.

CHAPTER III..166-179
Circumstances surrounding Andrew Jackson's marriage.—My visit to the noted battle grounds at New Orleans.—Story of Jackson's great victory.—Some high offices to which he had been appointed.—A brief review of his childhood.

PETER CARTWRIGHT.

CHAPTER I..180-183
Mr. Cartwright's successful efforts to defeat slavery.—His removal to Illinois in 1824.

CHAPTER II...184-186
Mr. Cartwright as a great preacher and a great organizer.—The Jacksonville Ordinance and how Mr. Cartwright assisted in its enforcement.

CHAPTER III..187-192
The name of Peter Cartwright familiar throughout the state.—His efforts to drive out the Mormons.—Grand ovation tendered him in 1869.—His labors at eighty-six years of age.—An incident of his last missionary tour.

AUTOBIOGRAPHY.

My Autobiography Briefly Sketched.................193-199

My ancestors, the Ross and Lee families.—Their descendants and some of their deeds.—The journey of my family from New York to Illinois.—Some of my early personal adventures.—My marriage to Jane R. Kirkpatrick, January 1st, 1840.—My personal work in the early development of the country.—The offices held and my work as a delegate to the National Prohibition convention in the year 1884.—The sixty years of my membership in the Presbyterian church.

Pioneer Times.

LIFE IN FULTON COUNTY SEVENTY TO EIGHTY YEARS AGO.*

CHAPTER I.

PIONEER JOURNEY FROM NEW YORK TO ILLINOIS.—THE PIROGUE OF THE EARLY SETTLER.—DR. DAVISON, THE "HERMIT," THE FIRST SETTLER.

OAKLAND, CAL., May 18, 1897.

MR. W. T. DAVIDSON:

I received your letter asking me to write for The Fulton Democrat a series of sketches on the early settlement of Fulton county. I have received similar requests from some of my relatives and old friends. There are no people in the wide world that I have as great a regard for as the people of Illinois, and no people for whom I feel the love and affection that goes from my heart to the pioneer of Fulton county. It was there that I spent the greater part of my boyhood and manhood; it was there where five of my children was born and raised, and where many of my relatives now live. There is such a warm place in my heart for the old settlers of Fulton county that it will be a pleasure for me to write these sketches. I hope they will add something to their knowledge and pleasure.

But in going into the early history of the county I will be compelled to allude very often to some of my relatives who were prominent as early settlers.

So I will commence with my father, Ossian M. Ross,

---

* Fulton County then comprising nearly the entire northern half of Illinois; now divided into fifty counties.

who with my mother, my brother Lewis, my sister Harriet and myself moved from Seneca county, New York, and settled on the quarter section of land just north of the present city of Lewistown in April, 1821.

My father was an officer in the war of 1812, and drew a half section of land; he settled upon one of the quarters, and on the other quarter he laid out the present city of Lewistown.

The family left New York in the fall of 1819 and went to Pittsburg, Pa., where he bought a small keel boat on which he loaded his household goods and other properties, and went down the Ohio river to its conjunction with the Mississippi river where Cairo now stands. Here the boat was frozen up in the ice, and we remained prisoners there until the next spring. Then we went up the Mississippi river to where the city of Alton now stands. There we left the boat and went back into the country about ten miles, near the town of Edwardsville, where my father rented a farm. He bought some horses, cows and other stock, and during the summer of 1821 raised a good crop. After the crops had been secured we went back to Alton where the keel boat had been left in charge of the ferryman, and loaded upon the boat all our household goods and family, and started up the river to our future home. Our hired men drove the wagon and stock across the country. Before we started into the wilderness of Fulton county my father went to St. Louis and laid in a supply of such articles as he thought we would need in our wilderness home. Among the other things was a good supply of flour and salt, guns and ammunition. He also bought a surveyor's compass and chain. He went to the surveyor general's office in St. Louis and got a sectional map of the Military Tract, which embraced all the land lying between the Mississippi and Illinois rivers and extended as far north as to include Bureau and Henry counties. He also got from the surveyor's office a copy of the field notes of the survey of the Military Tract that was made about three years before. These field notes were of very great importance to him and to many other early settlers in the county, as they enabled them to locate their lands by means of well established township and section corners, all clearly described in these field notes. Without them it would have been impossible for the people to have accurately located their land.

The little keel boat that we came up the river in was propelled by a sail when the wind was fair, and at other times by oars and poles. We were two weeks coming from Alton to the mouth of Spoon river at Havana, and the team and stock that were driven across the country arrived a few days later. We ran the boat up Spoon river to where John Eveland was living. He had settled there a year before.

My father on examining his map found that his land was about six miles north of Mr. Eveland's place. He took some of his men, and with his compass, chain and field notes he had no trouble in locating his land. The family staid on the boat until the team and stock arrived, and then we all moved onto our land. Father selected the quarter section north of Lewistown for our home, and built a log house on the east side of a little creek that ran through the land and near to a fine, large spring of water. The location was some sixty rods northeast from Major Walker's present residence. We lived there four years, and then built another log house where Major Walker now lives. We staid there until the fall of 1828, and then moved to Havana. Three years after my father sold the farm to Mahlon Winans, my mother's brother, for $1000.

The only white inhabitant in that part of the country at that time was John Eveland, who lived on the north side of Spoon river about a mile above where Waterford now stands, and Dr. W. T. Davison, who lived on the south side of the river a little higher up. Mr. Eveland had a large family of nine or ten children, part of them grown. They had some twenty acres in cultivation, and were engaged in raising stock. They had come into this country from Calhoun county, making the trip up the Illinois and

Spoon rivers, partly by land and partly by water. Before leaving Calhoun county they constructed a large pirogue (a large canoe). It was hewed out of a large cottonwood tree. The length of the boat was forty feet, and was about four feet wide. It was run by sail and also by oars. On this craft they shipped their hogs and part of their goods. These were the first hogs that were ever brought to Fulton county and were all of a red color.

This pirogue is entitled to more particular attention, because it was put to many uses of convenience and utility among the early settlers. It was the first craft used to carry people across the Illinois river at the mouth of Spoon river, and it was the craft that the Phelpses used in shipping their first stock of goods from St. Louis to Lewistown, and this was the first stock of goods ever brought to Fulton county. This pirogue was also put in use by the early settlers to run down Spoon river to the Illinois river, and thence down the Illinois river to the mouth of the Sangamon river, and thence up the Sangamon to Sangamontown, where there was a water-mill to which our people took their grain to be ground into breadstuff. A great skill had been used in digging out and constructing this pirogue. For years it took the place of the magnificent steamboat and railway trains that later generations employed.

John Eveland built a mill run by horse power where he settled on Spoon river which was the first mill built and operated in the county of Fulton. Some four or five years after he came to the county he moved and settled five miles southeast of Canton, and there built another horse mill.

Dr. Davison, who had settled on the south side of Spoon river a little west of the Eveland place, lived alone and was called "The Hermit." I could never learn where he came from nor when he settled in Fulton county. He had a good, comfortable cabin and a bearing peach orchard, which showed he had lived there for several years. He was doubtless the first settler in this part of Illinois.

The next settlers that settled in that country were two

brothers named Reuben and Roswell Fenner. They were both single men, and had come from Calhoun county upon the Illinois river in canoes and settled on the south side of Spoon river about two miles above Waterford. About a year after they settled there, Reuben, the oldest, was married to a Miss Rowley, whose father was a newcomer there. These two Fenners were the first persons ever incarcerated in the Lewistown jail, and it was for the crime of whipping to death of Reuben's wife, the particulars of which I will give in my next communication.

In 1822 a great many people began to move into Fulton county, but most of them came over from Sangamon county. They had come from eastern and southern states with the intention of settling in the Military Tract, but the country was full of Indians—indeed they could be counted by the thousands. The Sangamon river was about the dividing line between the white settlers and the Indians; so these men were afraid to venture over. But after Mr. Eveland and my father and a few other families had lived among the Indians a year or two and none of them had been butchered or scalped the people began to come to the county in great droves. The first settlements were made about Lewistown and Waterford.

In my next letter I will give the names of some of the other pioneers and will also tell what the Fenner boys whipped Mrs. Reuben Fenner to death for, and how they broke jail and got away, and of the excitement that it caused throughout the county.

CHAPTER II.

THE FIRST MURDER AMONG EARLY PIONEERS.—THE FIRST LAWYERS.—SOME ERRORS IN CHAPMAN'S HISTORY OF FULTON COUNTY.

There had been no circumstance ever occurred before in Fulton county that caused so much excitement and indignation as the murder of Mrs. Reuben Fenner by her husband and his brother. It was the first murder that took place in the county after the white people had settled it, and the Fenners were the first prisoners that ever occupied the new log jail.

Reuben and Roswell Fenner were both about six feet two inches tall, and were of such dark complexion as to suggest that they were part Indian. It was said by people in Calhoun county, where they came from, that there was Indian blood in them. They settled on the south side of Spoon river near the site of the celebrated Duncan Mills, afterwards erected four miles southwest of Lewistown. They built a log house and lived together alone. After they had lived there some eighteen months a man named Rowley came into the country and settled about a mile from the Fenners. The Rowleys had a daughter about twenty-two years old and a son aged ten or twelve. They had only lived there a few months when Reuben Fenner and Miss Rowley were married. He took her to their joint cabin. It turned out that Reuben was willing that his brother Roswell should share equally with him in his wife's affections, and that she rebelled with shame and indignation. Then the trouble commenced. She fought for her honor as any noble woman would do, but the poor girl was at the mercy of two heartless giants.

Her mother heard that she was sick in bed and went to see her, and the girl told her mother how both the brothers had whipped her and how cruelly they had treated her.

The young wife continued to grow worse, and in a few days died. When the word came to Lewistown of her death a great many of the people, both men and women, went down to the Fenner place to attend the funeral. When the people assembled they discovered that the Fenners had made a rough box for a coffin and had put her in it ready for burial. But the men opened the box and took the body out and examined it. They found many black stripes on her limbs and bruises on her body, and they decided that she had come to her death from cruel treatment at the hands of the Fenners. The Fenners were arrested and taken to the Lewistown jail. They had been confined for a couple of months waiting for the circuit court to convene, when one night some of their friends came and assisted them to escape. The jail was built of hewed logs twelve inches square, and a crowbar had been used to pry out the end of one of the logs so that they could crawl out. The next morning an officer went in pursuit of them, but they had gone to their cabin and loaded their goods into canoes and gone down the river, and it was the last that was ever heard of them. It was thought that some of their friends in Calhoun county, where they came from, had come up and liberated them. If they had not escaped it is probable that they would have been hung.

The new jail stood about ten rods south of the place where the old court house was located. At that time school was being taught in the old log court house by Peter Wood. I can remember how the school boys used to go and look through the grates of the jail to see the Fenners when they were there, and how we used to crawl in and out of the hole between the logs which they crept through in escaping. These public buildings in the '20s were very primitive buildings that would cause much derision in these days.

Mr. Rowley, the father of the murdered girl, must not be confounded with the Rowley who moved into the settlement some years after, and who also had some daughters. The first Rowley, whose daughter married Fenner, was about fifty years old, and had at some period in his life met with a misfortune that had given him a stiff neck. He could not turn his head in any direction any more than if his neck had been marble. He was at one time the guest of my father during a term of the court. While the Fenners were in jail they explained this circumstance by saying that Rowley had at one time been hung by the neck by a mob for horse-stealing, but they took him down before he was quite dead; and that was what had injured his neck. Soon after the Fenners had escaped from jail, Rowley, with his wife and son, left this country. I heard that he had made a solemn vow when the Fenners got away that he would hunt them down and that their lives should pay the penalty for the life of his daughter.

Last week my brother Leonard, of Lewistown, sent me a copy of Chapman's History of Fulton County. In looking over it I find that the author makes mention of this Fenner case, and says that Judge Stephen Phelps of Lewistown defended him and insisted that according to law and the Scriptures a man had the right to chastise his wife. The writer is evidently in error, for the Fenners escaped and were never tried for their crime; while Judge Phelps was a merchant and did not practice law.

The first lawyers that practiced law in Lewistown were Mr. Caverly of Vandalia, Pew of Springfield, John Bogardus of Peoria and Hugh R. Coulter of Lewistown. W. C. Osborn and William Elliott were the next lawyers who came to Lewistown. Among the first settlers that came to Lewistown were my father's family, David W. Barnes, John Totten, John Wolcott, Stephen Chase, John Jewell, Peter White, A. M. Williams, Lyman Tracy, David Gallatine, Stephen Dewey, Elijah Wentworth, John Holcomb, Robert Grant, George Matthews, Thomas Covell, Peter Cook and William Higgins. Then came my father's mother, Abigail Ross, and his three brothers, Joseph, Thomas and John, and his two brothers-in-law, Simeon Kelsey (father to Capt. William Phelps' first wife) and Hugh R. Coulter.

In looking over Chapman's History of Fulton County I find a great deal of very valuable information in it, and

I think he is entitled to the thanks of the people of Fulton county for getting up so good a work. But I have found some errors in it, and some of these I may have occasion to mention as I proceed with my narrative, for what the people want are the real facts. A history that does not contain the truth is no history at all.

There was another remarkable tragedy in the early settlement of the county that caused a great deal of talk and excitement among the people. It was the death of an old gentleman, Peter White. He is mentioned in Chapman's history as being one of the first petit jurymen chosen in the county. He was murdered, and his son, aged twenty-four, was arrested and charged with the murder. I will give the circumstances of this terrible tragedy in my next letter.

CHAPTER III.

TRAGICAL DEATH OF PETER WHITE.—THE ROSS FERRY.— A FIGHT BETWEEN PIONEERS AND INDIANS.

In regard to the tragical death of Peter White, supposed to have been murdered by his son, I will have to make a preliminary statement. When my father first came to the mouth of the Spoon river, in 1821, he determined, if possible, that he would be the owner of a ferry across the Illinois river at that place as soon as possible. It was forty miles down the river to the first ferry at Beardstown, and fifty miles to Peoria, where the next ferry was kept. He believed that it would be but a few years until there would be a good deal of travel across the river at Havana, and that a ferry at that place would be a paying investment. He was on the alert, and as soon as a license for a ferry could be procured he got one. It proved to be a good enterprise. For a good many years the receipts from the ferry amounted to about $2,000 a year.

Peter White came to Lewistown among the early settlers. He was fifty years old, was a widower, and had one son, a large, stout young man twenty-three or twenty-four years old, and his name also was Peter. They had worked about Lewistown and the old gentleman had worked for my father on the farm. He was an eastern man of good information, and a reliable man to work. My father made a bargain with both of them to go down to the river and keep the ferry and to put up a house where Havana now stands, as there was no house there at that time. My father rigged them out with a horse to haul the logs together, with tools, and some provisions to live on, and they started for the river. He also secured from John Eveland the pirogue alluded to last week to be used until the ferry boat could be built. The Whites first erected a little shanty to live in until they could cut the timber and make the clapboards for the house. So everything appeared to start off all right. After they had been down about six weeks young Peter came up to Lewistown one evening a little after dark, and staid at my father's all night. The next morning my father asked how he and his father were getting along with the house. "Not very well," was his reply. "Has anything gone wrong?" asked my father. "Yes, my father is dead," replied young Peter. On being asked what was the matter with his father, he coolly said that he and his father were working on the house and that his father had slipped and fallen off the house, and that his head struck a log lying near, and that it had broken his skull, resulting in his death. My father asked the boy what he had done with his father's body. He replied that he had dug a grave and wrapped him in a blanket, and put him on a sled and hauled him out and buried him.

The remarkable story that Peter told and the manner in which he had conducted himself made my father suspicious; so he went into Lewistown to confer with others as to what had better be done. It was not long until old John Eveland came up from Spoon river, and he reported that Peter had come to his house the day before, had taken dinner with them, had played ball, had run foot-races, and shot at a mark with his boys, but had not said a word about his father's death. So my father and Mr. Eveland and three or four others concluded to go down to the river, and take Peter along, and investigate the matter. He took them to the grave where he had buried his father. They got a spade and dug open the grave, took up the body, and examined it. They found a spot on the side of the head where the skull had been broken from a blow by some blunt instrument. They then went to the house which Peter said his father had fallen from. There was no logs near the house on which he could have struck his head, and the house had only been raised six or seven feet, so that a fall from it was not likely to kill a man. Some ten feet away was a pile of logs, with a couple of handspikes lying upon them which had been used in handling the logs. All of the men were of the opinion that the old man had come to his death from a blow struck by Peter with one of those handspikes. They believed that Peter and his father had quarreled about something, and that Peter in a passion had struck his father with a handspike, but with no intention of killing him; but that the blow had proved fatal.

As the supposed murder had occurred in Sangamon county it was decided that the best thing to do was to send Peter to Springfield, and a couple of men agreed to take him there and deliver him to the sheriff. The other men returned to their homes. The next day the two men came back to Lewistown and reported that Peter had gotten away from them. It was the general belief that they had given Peter a good whipping and let him go. But that was the last that was ever heard of him in that country.

The next parties that my father got to take charge of the ferry were Norman and Ira Scoville, two brothers. They finished the house that the Whites had commenced to build, and also built another log house near by. These men staid two or three years, when Norman Scoville engaged to run a keel boat for the Phelpses, and then my father rented the ferry property to Samuel Mallory and Wm. Nicholls. They were keeping the ferry and the tavern at the time the fight took place between the Indians and the whites as recorded in Chapman's history, page 205. The author has made some mistakes in regard to material facts. He says the fight took place in 1828 at Mallory's ferry, and that the whites proved to be the victors. This is all wrong. The battle took place in 1826, and the ferry was never called Mallory's ferry, but was Ross' ferry. No man named Mallory ever kept the ferry, and the Indians were the victors in the fight. The true history of that fight is as follows: As I have already stated, Samuel Mallory and his stepson, Wm. Nicholls, had rented the ferry of my father. They were both old settlers of Fulton county. Mallory was the father of Hirah Saunders' wife and the grandfather of Mrs. Judge H. L. Bryant. A few years later he and Nicholls settled some eight miles south of Canton on the Lewistown road.

After they had been at the river a few weeks they received by keel boat a barrel of whisky from St. Louis. At that time all tavern keepers were expected to keep liquor for the accommodation of their guests. In fact, almost every merchant in the country kept whisky for sale as freely as any other kind of goods. A party of Indians were travelling up the Illinois river in their canoes and camped a half mile above the ferry. They came down to the house to trade some furs for whisky, as they had been in the habit of doing with the Scovilles. But Mallory refused to let them have any whisky. As he was alone they drew their tomahawks over his head and compelled him to give them whisky. Wm. Nicholls, who had been out working in the woods, came home, and seeing the situation Mallory was in, slipped away and got into a canoe and slipped across the river to where the keel boat was lying. But part of the boat crew had started off for Lewistown. He hurried on and overtook them, and told them the situation that Mallory was in. So each one of them cut a stout hickory cane and went back with him to rescue Mallory. They found that some twenty-five Indians had Mallory completely under their control. Some of them were pretty drunk and all were having a jolly time except Mallory. The white men ordered the Indians to leave, but they refused to go, and then the fight commenced, the white men using their hickory canes on the heads of the Indians. But the Indians were about four to one, and they succeeded in getting the canes away from the white men. It was a pretty hot fight for about half an hour, and the whites would probably have whipped the Indians, but while they were in the fight they saw some squaws coming from the canoes with Indian spears and tomahawks for the use of the Indians. Then the whites thought it was about time to retreat and get more help. As they were hurrying to the ferry boat they discovered Simeon Kelsey and a couple of Indians having a hard fight near the river, and in attempting to capture the Indians one of the Indians ran into the river and they took after him with the ferry boat, and when they would get near him he would dive under the water and come up a rod or two behind the boat and would be making for the shore. The white men would then have to turn their boat and go after him again; he would play the same game of dodging them; they kept up this chase for about half an hour, when they came upon him where they could see his head two feet under the water. One of the men ran his arm down and caught him by the hair, and as he drew his head over the side of the boat another man drew his knife and cut the Indian's throat, leaving him to sink in the river.

The men returned to the keel boat and Wm. Nicholls started to Lewistown for more men to fight the Indians. He got there after dark, raised the alarm, and the next morning fifteen men on horseback started for the battle-field. I will give the result of their expedition in my next letter.

CHAPTER IV.

THE ENDING OF THE INDIAN FIGHT.—MY BOYHOOD GHOST FOR AN INDIAN SCARE.—MY FATHER'S TRADE WITH THE INDIANS.—EARLY RELIGIOUS CUSTOMS OF THE INDIANS.—A WAR DANCE.

To continue the story of the Indian fight as described last week: The company of men raised in Lewistown numbered fifteen, all on horseback and each with a gun. Among those in the company were Robert Grant, John Jewell, Wm. Johnson, John and Wm. Nicholls, Moses Freeman, Isaac Benson, O. M. Ross and Edward Plude. Freeman and Benson had come a few weeks before from the East, and were engaged at the time in putting the counters and shelves in a store room for my father that stood on the Harris corner in Lewistown. Plude was a Frenchman, and kept store in a frame house where Ewan's hardware store now stands.

When the company got to the Illinois river at Havana they were joined by the keel-boat crew that had had the fight with the Indians the day before, with the exception of Kelsey, who had been badly used up in the fight and was not able to go with them. The men all got on the ferry boat and took as many horses as they could crowd on the boat, and started across the river. Some squaws a little way down the river saw the men coming; they ran up the bank and told the Indians that a great company of white men were coming with guns. Plude understood the Indian language, and knew what the squaws said to the Indians. The Indians instantly took the alarm and started on the run. Some went to their canoes and poled off up the river, and some ran to the woods. The men followed the Indians that ran to the woods until they got into the swamps and marshes a few miles up the river, and then they had to give up the chase.

The company came back to Mallory's house where the

fight had taken place the day before. They found some pools of blood, and a short distance away they found two new-made graves, showing that the fight had been a hard one and that at least two Indians had been killed with clubs besides the one whose throat was cut on the ferry boat. They also found that no more than eight or ten gallons of whisky had been taken from Mallory's barrel, and that his household goods had not been touched. So that ended the fight of Ross' ferry for that time.

Mallory and Nicholls kept the ferry for about a year after that and never had any further trouble with the Indians. My father then moved to Havana and took charge of the ferry himself.

The Indian that had his throat cut floated down the river and landed in some driftwood at the head of an island three miles below Havana. We had often heard the hunters tell of the Indian's bones lying in the driftwood there. At that time was living with my father John Herriford, who was so long a resident at Bernadotte, and he was well known to many of the pioneers of Fulton county. One Sunday John went down to the island and brought up the Indian's skull and jawbone. As soon as I saw them I decided to have a good deal of sport in frightening the Indians, who were very superstitious. I thoroughly cleaned the skull and jawbone, and fastened them on a jackstaff about four feet long, sharpened at the lower end to be stuck into the ground. I then fixed the skull so that I could put into it a lighted candle. When the scarecrow was set up of a dark night, with the candle lighted and shining out of the eye-sockets, ears, nose, and through the gleaming white teeth, it was certainly the most terrifying object mortal ever beheld. About a mile above Havana there were eighteen or twenty wigwams of Indians, and they were in the habit of coming to town every week to do some trading, and would frequently stay until after dark before starting home. I knew the path they traveled and would have the ghost set up a few rods from their path. When they would discover my hideous ghost they would start on the run as fast as their legs could carry them, frightened nearly into convulsions. It made a great commotion among the Indians for awhile, but my father found out what was going on and put a sudden stop to all my fun. One day a steamboat landed at the wharf and I went down to it with my scarecrow. The pilot paid me $2 for the outfit to put upon the bow of his boat at night to scare the natives along the river.

Soon after my father went to Havana he built three warehouses, one on the east side of the river and two on the west side. One of these was north of Spoon river, and the other on the south side. They were built of hewed logs and were used to store the produce of farmers and the merchandise of the merchants who lived on both sides of the river. The upper part of the warehouse on the Havana side of the river he finished off for a store and opened therein a stock of goods. The nearest stores to him was at Lewistown, twelve miles away on the west, and New Salem, twenty-five miles east. The Phelpses had established a trading post, two years before, on Grand Island, nine miles below Havana; but when my father opened his store they closed out their business on the island and moved to Yellowbanks (now Oquawka) on the Mississippi river.

My father had a large trade with the Indians, for they were scattered all over the country up and down the Illinois river and both sides of the Spoon river. Their wigwams could be counted by the hundreds. About the mouth of Spoon river was a great resort for their Indian ponies. Hundreds of them would be brought there every fall to feed on the grass that kept green all winter; and if there was a deep snow the Indians would chop down small trees for their ponies to browse upon until the snow went off. My father would often sell them goods on a credit of six months, but would require a recommendation from some of their chiefs, which made them very punctual to pay their debts. The Indians were very numerous in all that country until in 1832 when the Black Hawk war broke out and they all went west.

These Indians at a certain stage of the moon each fall held a great religious festival on the island just in front of Havana. It was then a very heavily timbered and picturesque spot. The Indians would congregate there in hundreds, and their religious rites and ceremonies would last four days. They had an abundance of good things to eat, and put in much of the time singing and dancing. One of their ceremonies was to burn a live dog to death. They would select a small white dog and make his feet fast with four wooden pins which they would drive in the ground, and then pile wood and brush over him until he was covered four or five feet deep. They would set fire to the pile and then gather in a ring about it. When the dog would commence to burn he would set up the most terriffic and awful howling that was ever heard. His cries would ring through the woods for half a mile. When the dog would commence howling, the Indians would set up some doleful and dismal dirge and keep it up as long as the dog kept howling. Then followed a war-dance, and that would be the end of the festival. My brother Leonard was present at one time when they made a sacrifice of a little dog. He was only about seven or eight years old, but when the little dog made such a terrible yelping he wanted to clean out the whole Indian tribe.

There were many singular customs and tragic events relating to these Indians that I may detail as I proceed with my narrative.

CHAPTER V.

AN EARLY PIONEER DANCE.—MAJOR NEWTON WALKER AND HIS FIDDLE.—A PIONEER WAGON RIDE.

CORRECTION—Hon. Inman Blackaby says Mr. Ross is in error in his statement in Chapter III, that "Samuel Mallory was the father of Hirah Saunders' wife, and grandfather to Mrs. H. L. Bryant." The fact is that Mrs. Hirah Saunders was a step-daughter to Samuel Mallory—a full sister to Wm. K. Nicholls also alluded to by Mr. Ross. Mr. Blackaby lived with W. K. Nicholls in 1846, and Mr. Mallory and his wife were living with them at that time. Mr. Blackaby taught school in that district and boarded with these people part of the time. Mr. Ross' letters will doubtless go into a future history of Fulton county. He will join the editor of The Democrat in thanking pioneers for similar corrections as to any fact.

In The Democrat of June 10 I find the story related by Major Newton Walker about his fiddling at our Havana ball sixty years ago. He has always been noted for his accurate memory, but in this case he has forgotten some of the incidents. It will interest young people to know about the pioneer manner of conducting parties. It was Dr. Price, and not Dr. Allen, who went with me to Lewistown to secure the services of Major Walker as our fiddler. Dr. Price then lived in Havana, but afterwards moved to Lewistown. Dr. Hillburt was also a Havana doctor. When the Major agreed to go with us we called for him at Truman Phelps' tavern in a common two-horse wagon. He was evidently expecting a carriage, but was too polite to say anything. The only seat was a board laid across the wagon bed. The Major came out with his violin in a beautiful case, and the case was wrapped up as carefully as if it had been a baby. We got on very well until we came to the bottom road beyond Waterford where heavy teaming had made deep ruts. The front wheels would occasionally drop into a deep rut, and down would go our seat with all three of us sprawling in the wagon bed. But we finally got to the ball-room, and the dance commenced much as the Major described it. The man who wanted him to play faster was Dr. Hillburt. He was very portly, and weighed some 200 pounds. After Hillburt had danced about half an hour, he pulled off his coat; a little later away went his vest; and as he got warmer he kicked off his shoes and finished the "French four" in his stocking feet. In regard to the Major's comments on my dancing I have only to say that he had not lived long enough in Illinois to know what good Sucker dancing was! After the dance was over we took up a collection of about $10 to pay the fiddler, but Major Walker declined the money, and said he would only ask us to send him back to Lewistown. I can only say that if he had run for office he would have gotten every vote in Havana.

But he is in error in saying that it was the first time we had ever met. I remember very well when Col. Simms and Major Walker passed through Havana with their caravan from Virginia. They stayed with my father over night, and the next morning we ferried them over the Illinois river. They had the most splendid traveling outfit I had ever seen. Their horses were large and fine. They had several carriages and wagons, and one tremendous four-horse "prairie schooner." The wagon was about twenty feet long and eight feet high, and all heavily ironed off in old Virginia style. The ferryman said that it was the biggest wagon that had ever crossed the river.

About two months later I took a carriage and a light pair of horses to drive my mother over to Lewistown to visit her brother, Mahlon Winans, who then lived where Major Walker now lives. Three or four miles out of Lewistown one of our axletrees was broken. We then made our way afoot to the cabin of Nathaniel Bordwine (still living in Lewistown), hoping to get a wagon from him, but it was in Lewistown. I left mother at the cabin and with my horses went on to Mr. McGeehee's farm, but his wagon was not at home. Thence I went on to Minard Van Dyke's, then to Dr. Rice's, and then to George Bennett's, but their wagons were away or busily employed. Lastly I went to Hiram Wentworth's place (just east of Lewistown), sure that I would get a wagon there. When I rode up to the house the

first thing that struck my attention was a strapping big
negro at work in the yard, and in the lane stood the mighty
"prairie schooner" we had ferried across the river. Major
Walker came to the door and told me that he had bought
the Wentworth place. I told him of my predicament; but
Col. Simms had driven the carriage into town, and there
was not a wagon on the place except the huge four-horse
one. I could not wait for the carriage, as a storm was
brewing; so with the negro's help I hitched my two little
horses onto the big wagon. The stiff tongue stuck six feet
out ahead of them, and when I climbed into the wagon the
front end-gate came up to my chin. The big negro said to
me: "Young massa, what y'er goin' to do wid dat big wagon?" I told him that I was going to take a lady a riding. It
tickled him tremendously, and as I drove away he stood
with his mouth spread and nearly in convulsions of laughter. He had doubtless seen many strange things, but to
take a lady riding in a four-horse wagon was too much for
him.

And so I drove back in state to get mother. Fortunately, there was a high rail fence at Mr. Bordwine's; so mother
climbed the high fence and so got into the wagon. [Mrs.
Ross was very fleshy.—Ed.] There was a huge chain on
each side of the wagon, and at each hill I had to climb out
and lock the wheels to keep the big wagon from running
over my little horses. We fortunately arrived in Lewistown after dark, and escaped the astonished gaze of the
people. But when we got to Uncle Winans' there was no
high fence, and no ladder. It was a profound problem as
to how we would ever get mother out of her chariot. But
finally a common wagon was run up close to the big one,
and by the aid of a high chair we managed to get her safely
to earth. The next day mother sent me back with the big
wagon to Major Walker, and gave me a half dollar to pay
for its use. But I said it was such a big wagon the price
might be more. So she gave me another fifty cents. When
I drove out, there stood that big negro in the same spot, his
mouth wide open, laughing, just as I had left him, giving
me the impression that my joke had paralyzed him the

night before. But I gave him the dollar to pay Major Walker. He soon came out and said: "De folks say der ain't no charge, and you'm pufeely welcome to de wagin."

CHAPTER VI.

THE FIRST LOG HOUSES, THEIR CONSTRUCTION.—OLD-FASHIONED FIREPLACE; THE LATCH-STRING; THE HOMINY MORTAR; THE REAP-HOOK AND FLAIL.—THE FIRST HORSE MILL OF THE EARLY SETTLER.—"SQUAW CORN." —MY MOTHER'S RESCUE OF HER KETTLE FROM THE INDIANS, WITH HER FIRE-SHOVEL.

As stated in my first letter, my father moved his family from New York to Fulton county, Illinois, in 1821, locating on his farm just north of the city of Lewistown. The country was at that time a vast wild wilderness, covered by majestic trees, and Indian wigwams were scattered thickly all over the wilderness. The only indications that white men had ever before penetrated the country were the marks and numbers on occasional trees, the handiwork of a company of surveyors who had surveyed the land some two or three years earlier. Our nearest white neighbors were six miles away on Spoon river; the next nearest at Rushville, thirty miles south; and on the north the nearest white inhabitants were at Fort Clark, now Peoria, fifty miles distant.

The first thing to be done on our arrival at our wilderness home, was to build a log house. The younger people will be interested to know how it was built, and how we commenced life in the wilderness. The first house my father built was 20 x 24 feet in size and one story high. We cut trees of uniform size for the logs, and the ends of each log were "saddled," or notched, so as to bring the logs as near together as possible. The cracks between them were "chinked," or filled with small slabs, and then daubed with mud inside and out. It made as solid a wall as brick and mortar. The gables were made of logs gradually shortened to the comb. The roof was made of small logs laid from gable to gable; on these were laid clapboards, and these were fastened down by logs laid upon each row, there being no nails. These outside logs were held in place by laying pieces of timber between them. A wide chimney-place was cut out of one end of the cabin, and the chimney built outside of the house. It was built of rived sticks put up cob-house fashion and plastered inside and out with clay mortar. The fire-place was made large enough to take in a four-foot back-log. The floors were made of puncheons hewed smooth on one side; the doors of split boards, shaved with a drawing-knife, and hung with wooden hinges. The door was opened by pulling a leather latch-string which raised a wooden latch inside the door. For security at night the latch-string was pulled in, then there was no way to open the door from the outside. After the house was built the first thing that was done was to break up twenty acres of land, and fence it, and plant it in corn and vegetables, and in the fall we put in ten acres of wheat. As soon as the corn got hard enough to grate, a grater was prepared by taking a piece of tin and piercing it with a great number of holes, and then bending it over a piece of short board. With this simple instrument the corn was rubbed into meal. It made very good bread and was most excellent for mush. As soon as the corn got hard enough to pound, a hominy mortar was made. This was done by burning a hole in one end of a log or in the top of a stump large enough to hold a peck of corn. Then we had a wooden pestle which was suspended by a spring-pole to lessen the labor; and with this pestle and mortar the grains of corn were crushed into excellent meal. Another way we had of preparing our corn was by scalding it with strong lye made from wood ashes until the husk was eaten off by the alkali, and then washing the corn in clean water until all traces of the husk and taste of the lye were removed. This was the old-fashioned hominy, and made a very good substitute for bread. When our wheat was ripe we cut it with a sickle, or a reap-hook, and then thrashed it out with a flail or tramped it out with horses, winnowed it with a sheet, ground it in a horse-mill, bolted it with a hand-bolt and then baked it in a Dutch oven.

After we had lived in the county about a year, John Eveland, who lived on Spoon river six miles south of us, built a horse-mill, which was the first mill built in Fulton county. I remember very well of riding on a horse behind my brother Lewis when he took a grist of corn to Eveland's mill to be ground into meal. The fact of riding twelve miles on a bare-back, hard-trotting horse made an impression not only on my mind, but also on my legs, that I did not soon forget, for I was so sore that I could scarcely walk for two days. So I am not mistaken about where the first mill was built, although Chapman's History of Fulton County says the first mill was built in Fulton county by O. M. Ross at Lewistown. About a year after that time my father did build a horse-mill, which was the second mill built in the county. It was located about half way between my father's house and Lewistown. The county road from Lewistown to Canton at that time ran on the east side of Spudaway creek and a few rods west of where the C. B. & Q. railroad now runs, and ran by my father's house, located about eighty rods northeast of Major Walker's present residence. In about four years my father moved to the spot where Major Walker's house now stands and the road (Main street) was changed to its present location. When my father built the mill he also erected a blacksmith shop under the same roof which was carried on by Jacob Niman, who came from Edwardsville, Illinois, with my father. I shall have more to say of him and his wife as I proceed with my story.

As I have already said, the country was full of Indians. One could not travel in any direction without coming across Indian wigwams. Six or eight families would congregate together near some creek or spring of water, and the squaws would fence three or four acres of land, and dig up the ground, and plant it in corn and beans. Those were the principal crops that they raised. The Indian men seldom did anything but hunt. The squaws did all the hard work. The corn they raised was of a dark blue color and the beans a dark red. The kernels were large and plump, and both corn and beans were of a very early variety. Our people procured some of the seed to plant in our garden for early use and raised both corn and beans for several years. We named the corn "Squaw Corn." The squaws fenced in their ground by setting small posts about ten feet apart and tying to them small poles with hickory bark or strings cut from deerskin. They would have only two or three poles to the panel, for the Indian ponies were the only kind of stock they had to fear. But when the white people came in with their cattle and hogs the Indians would either move further out in the wilderness or would build better fences. When we came and settled amongst them the Indians were very friendly, and I think they were pleased to have us come. When they were kindly treated they showed no disposition to molest or hurt the white people. They had a strong propensity to steal and pilfer, and would pick up any thing they could find and carry it away, so we had to be constantly on our guard when they were around. About eighteen months after we moved on our farm an Indian and two squaws came to our house to trade some maple sugar for some flour. The Indians at that time made considerable maple sugar, and we were in the habit of getting our sugar from them. The men of our family were all out in the field at work, and there was no one at home but my mother and old Mrs. Niman, my sister Harriet, myself and our little sister Lucinda, who was then about a year old. While mother was measuring out the sugar and flour one of the Indian squaws stole her brass kettle and secreted it under the skirts of her dress. My mother brought the kettle from New York and prized it very highly. She had been using it just before the Indians came in, and as there had been no other person in the house, she knew very well that one of them had stolen it. So she told the Indians that they must give her back her kettle. They positively denied knowing anything about it, and were starting to go out of the house when my mother seized our long-handled iron shovel, sprang to the door and closed it, and told them they could not go until they gave up the kettle. They still denied having it. My mother then ordered them to take off their blankets, for they all wore blankets. The Indian took off his blanket and showed that he did not have the kettle; then one of the squaws took off her blanket, and showed that she was innocent; when the other squaw took off her blanket mother could plainly see the outline of the kettle under her skirt. Mother pointed to it and told her to take it out, so the squaw unhooked the kettle from under her dress and gave it to mother, when the Indians were permitted to depart. Mother very well knew that if they got out of the house with the kettle she would never see it again. Her intention was if the Indians did not give up the kettle to hold the Indians there with the big iron shovel until she could send one of the children to the field for the men. The pioneer fire-shovel was a very heavy and formidable weapon. The women had to do all their cooking in a fire-place, as cooking-stoves were then unknown; and the iron shovel they used to stir up the log fire and to put coals of fire on their bake oven had an iron handle three feet long and the shovel part was maybe six inches square, weighing a pound or so. It would have been a serious thing coming in contact with an Indian's head. We had many other little conflicts with the Indians, arising usually out of their tendency to steal, and I may mention some of them as I proceed with my narrative.

CHAPTER VII.

THE NIMANS.—FIRST BLACKSMITH SHOP OPENED BY JACOB NIMAN.—DR. CHARLES NEWTON, A CELEBRATED PIONEER PHYSICIAN.—ANOTHER ERROR IN CHAPMAN'S HISTORY.

When my father moved to Fulton county he brought with him a man and wife. His name was Jacob Niman. He found them at Edwardsville, where we had spent a year in preparation for coming to our wilderness home. They had walked all the way from Philadelphia, and wanted to go to the Military Tract. My father hired them, and they came with us up the river on the keel boat. Niman was a large, stout Dutchman and a blacksmith by trade. His wife was an Englishwoman, a good cook, an excellent seamstress, and could cut and make any kind of a garment from a pair of buckskin breeches to a lady's fine dress. In addition to these accomplishments she was a professional midwife. It made her a valuable acquisition to this new settlement, especially as there was not a doctor nearer than Springfield, fifty miles distant. Her services were frequently called for until Dr. Newton came to the county. Niman was a man of rare courage. We had bought of John Eveland a sow and litter of pigs and placed them in a rail pen near our house. One night Niman heard a terrible racket in the pigpen, and seizing a handspike he ran out to find a huge panther in the pen trying to kill the pigs. As Niman came up the panther tried to jump out of the pen, but he struck the animal on the head with the handspike and killed it.

Mr. Niman opened the first blacksmith shop in Fulton county. He died about in 1825, and was buried a few rods east of where the old Presbyterian church stood (now the little East school house. His bones are evidently lying in the ground occupied by some of the residents of Ross Place.) So Chapman's History has made a mistake of ten years in saying that Eastman Call opened the first blacksmith shop in Lewistown. Niman had the first. The second was opened by Harrison Huling, who afterwards went to Canton and opened the first blacksmith shop in that town. The third shop was opened by A. W. Williams, and Eastman Call may have come in fourth.

Mrs. Niman lived at my father's about five years. She was a faithful, good woman. She had left a son in Philadelphia bound out to learn the shoemaker's trade. He came to see her in 1821, but claimed to be a maker of fine boots and shoes, and was afraid the people of Lewistown would not patronize him very well, so he located in Springfield. Before my father went to Havana he deeded to Mrs. Niman a block of lots near where the C., B. & Q. depot now stands in Lewistown, and built her a house on the ground. The old inhabitants will remember the noble and kind-hearted old lady, Mrs. Jacob Niman, who was ever ready and willing to minister to the sick and sorrowful.

My father also brought with him from Edwardsville a man named Zweltin, who was a shoemaker, and a carpenter by the name of Enos—both good and reliable men.

One of the notable characters that settled in Lewistown in the early times was Dr. Charles Newton. He came from Green county, Illinois, and located in Lewistown in 1825. He was an Eastern man, had been well educated, and was considered a very good and skillful doctor. He was the only practicing physician in the county for about two years. He practiced all over the county where there was a settlement. He kept no regular office but made his home at my father's most of the time. He would occasionally take a drinking spree that would last a day or two, but aside from that he was as perfect a gentleman as any person could wish to have at their house. My father first met him at Vandalia and told him that he thought there was a good opening for a doctor in Lewistown; so he closed up his business and moved to Lewistown. He was a good deal attached to my father, and often said that there was no place that seemed like home except at our house. A year after we moved to Havana Dr. Newton came down to live with us. So he was the first doctor at Lewistown and the first at Havana.

While the doctor was living at our house in Havana my mother started me off one day to hunt up a girl to do our housework. I crossed the river and struck off into South Fulton, and every house I came to I enquired for girls. Finally I was directed to an old gentleman who lived down in the edge of Schuyler county, by the name of Louderback, who was said to have four girls. I found the place and told them my business, and the oldest one agreed to go with me. It was a long trip and we did not get home until late at night. The doctor had gone to bed, but he called me to his room and wanted to know what kind of a girl that was that I had brought home. I told him that she was a splendid, fine-looking girl. "Do you think," said he, "that she would make the doctor a good wife?" I replied that I thought she would make any man a good wife. So the doctor courted her, and in about three months they were married. Havana was at that time in Tazewell county, and Tremont was the county seat, fifty miles away. So the doctor had to get his license in Lewistown, and employed Esq. J. P. Boice of Lewistown to come down and marry them. As the marriage had to be performed in the county where the license was issued a crowd of some twenty-five or thirty of us, with Esq. Boice and the bride and groom, rowed out in the Illinois river in a boat until we were past the channel, so as to be in Fulton county, and the ceremony was performed on the boat. There was a young harness maker of Havana in the party who had been paying his attentions to Miss Louderback, and in fact was very much smitten with her, for she was indeed a very handsome and attractive young lady. When Esq. Boice was repeating the marriage ceremony, and came to the place that if any person had any objections why the said parties should not be bound in the holy bonds of matrimony to then let it be known or forever after to hold their peace, young Cook, who was sitting on the gunwale of the boat, rose up and said that he objected. The 'squire asked him what was his objections. He replied that he wanted the young lady himself. Esq. Boice told him that he did not think that was a legal objection, so went on and performed the marriage ceremony. The ferry boat was then rowed back to town, and all went to the Havana Hotel, where a wedding infair was given by the host and hostess, and the table was spread with the best that the country could afford. About three months later the doctor and his wife moved over into South Fulton where he practiced a couple of years, and then they moved up near the town of Cuba. Dr. Newton was appointed surgeon in the Black Hawk war. He was entitled to two servants, and had the right to draw pay for them the same as for himself. When the pay roll was being made out the officers asked the doctor what were the names of his two servants. He had no servants, but in order to draw pay for them he gave the names of George Baker and Truman Phelps. On being asked afterwards why he gave these two names, he said that they had served him more times than any other men he could think of. Each one kept a tavern and a bar, and it was at the bar that they had "served" him so faithfully. Truman Phelps was a very proud man and was terribly cut up at being officially rated as a servant.

Chapman's History says that Truman Phelps kept the first tavern in Fulton county. This is a mistake. George Baker kept a tavern in the brick house occupied by William Proctor (on the site of the Ewan hardware store), two years before Truman Phelps came to the country. While Dr. Newton was still living with my father in Lewistown word came that the wife of Capt. David Haacke was very sick and for the doctor to come and see her. He lived about six miles north of Lewistown. Big Creek had to be crossed, and at that time the waters were high. The doctor had been drinking some that day, and father was afraid for him to go alone; so he sent me along to see that the doctor got through all right. The doctor found his patient a very sick woman. He did the best he could for her, but in a few days she died. Some years after that Capt. Haacke became the owner of one of the finest farms between Canton and Cuba. After the death of Dr. Newton Capt. Haacke married the doctor's widow, and soon rented out his farm and moved to Canton. The last time I was in Canton, some eighteen years ago, I visited Capt. and Mrs. Haacke at their home, and I think they were the happiest couple I have ever met. So I think Capt. Haacke could agree with me in what I told Dr. Newton the evening that I brought the young lady to the hotel, that "she would make any man a good wife."

CHAPTER VIII.

PIKE COUNTY ORGANIZED.—FIRST ELECTION IN FULTON COUNTY HELD AT MY FATHER'S HOUSE.—MY FATHER'S VOTE THE FIRST CAST IN FULTON COUNTY.—JOHN L. BOGARDUS, ONE OF PEORIA'S EARLY SETTLERS.—FIRST MARRIAGES IN FULTON COUNTY.—MY SISTER LUCINDA THE FIRST WHITE CHILD BORN IN THIS TERRITORY.

The first county formed west of the Illinois and east of the Mississippi, and also embracing all North Illinois, was Pike, organized in 1821. The county seat was Cole's Grove, now in Calhoun county. In 1824 it was moved to Atlas, and in 1833 it went permanently to the fine little city of Pittsfield. The town of Atlas was laid out on a bluff three miles from the Mississippi river by the Ross brothers, who came to Illinois the year before my father came. They were John, William and Leonard; they were enterprising and excellent citizens and owned a good deal of land in that part of the state. They not only located the county seat to their liking, but subsequently preempted about all the local offices in that county. They were distant relatives of our family, having also come from Scotland. My father was so friendly with them that he named my brother Leonard for the one of that name. Some of the descendants of these Pike county Rosses now own fine fruit ranches in Santa Clara Valley, Cal.

The first probate court held in Pike county was in May, and the first circuit court in October, 1821, at Cole's Grove. The first probate judge was Abraham Beck; the first circuit judge, John Reynolds; first representative, Nicholas Hanson; first senator, Thos. Carlin. Carlin and Reynolds afterwards became, each, governor of Illinois.

The first election ever held near Lewistown was at my father's house Aug. 5, 1822, while we were still in Pike county. The judges of the election were Abner Eads, Stephen Chase and Reuben Fenner, and John Totten was the clerk. The candidates for governor at that election were Edward Coles, Joseph Phillips and Thomas C. Brown. Coles got nineteen; Phillips, seven; Brown, six. For congress, Daniel P. Cook got all the votes, thirty-three; for representative, Nicholas Hanson got thirteen votes; for sheriff, John Shaw eighteen, Leonard Ross twelve, and B. C. Fenton twenty; for coroner, Daniel Whipple twelve, James Bacon fifteen.

The first election ever held in Fulton county after its organization was also held at my father's house about three-quarters of a mile northeast of the Court House Square in Lewistown, on April 14, 1823. The boundaries of the county at that time extended from the Illinois river to the Mississippi and to the northern line of the state, including Galena, Chicago and all that country. The judges at that election were George Brown, Amos Eveland and Hazel Putnam; the clerks, Thos. Lee Ross and John Totten. There were no great national issues at that election, but it was run on local issues mainly. It was then—seventy-four years ago—just what it has ever been, North Fulton vs. South Fulton; and the fight was over the office of sheriff. The people of North Fulton had nominated for that office a man named Abner Eads of Peoria, and the people of South Fulton had nominated my father, Ossian M. Ross. The voters from the northern part of the county (all Northern Illinois) came down the Illinois river in canoes, then up Spoon river to Waterford, and then walked through the woods seven miles to my father's house where the election was held, for it was then the only voting precinct in all that majestic portion of Illinois now containing fifty counties, many hundreds of cities and towns, and people by the millions! It was a big battle like some of the later county seat fights in Fulton county. Eads and Ross had marshalled all their forces from Rushville on the south to Fort Clark (Peoria) and Chicago on the north. The North Fultonites had brought whiskey with them. In those days men could travel and hold elections without carrying much food, for they could live on game; but they could not get on without plenty of whiskey. When the election was over it was found that *thirty-five* (35) votes had been cast, and that Eads had beaten Ross by a majority of four votes! But it afterwards was shown that as Eads came down the river with his sixteen voters he stopped at "Town Site" (now Pekin) in Sangamon county, and brought with him two bachelors—fraudulent voters—and by this means won the election.

I have in my possession the original poll books of the elections of 1822 and 1823, just as they came from the hands of the judges and clerks of those elections. So I can tell exactly how every vote was cast. The poll book for 1823 shows that my father cast the first vote that was ever cast in Fulton county (all Northern Illinois), and it was cast for Abner Eads, his opponent for the office of sheriff. My uncle, Hugh R. Coulter, was the first county and circuit clerk, judge of probate and county recorder. My uncle, Thomas Lee Ross, was the first assessor and county treasurer. My uncle, John N. Ross, was the first surveyor. In 1824 my father was elected county treasurer and sheriff and was appointed the first postmaster in big Fulton county.

In regard to the first settlements and first towns built up in the territory I have described, Chicago had the start of the others, and Peoria was the next. But in 1830 they both fell behind some of the other towns. The towns of Atlas, Quincy, Columbus, Rushville, Lewistown, Peoria, Galena and Chicago would not, in 1830, have varied 200 in population, Lewistown being a little ahead of all the others. From the most reliable accounts to be had, Chicago in 1830 did not contain more than eighteen to twenty houses, and its population did not exceed 200. It was organized in 1833, and incorporated as a city in 1837.

One of the first settlers at Ft. Clark (Peoria) was John L. Bogardus. He went there in 1819. He was a lawyer, and he and Hugh R. Coulter were the first lawyers in Fulton county. Mr. Bogardus attended the first court terms held in Lewistown. He was a very energetic and successful business man. He owned most of the land that now constitutes Peoria and laid out the first town lots in that city. He also kept a ferry across the Illinois river at that place. One peculiar line of business he engaged in was the manufacture of fish oil, shipping it by boat to St. Louis. At the outlet of Peoria Lake in early times vast quantities of fish would congregate. He had them caught in vast quantities in seines, would throw them into huge hoppers holding several wagon loads, and leave them there to be tried out into oil under the fierce rays of the sun. He had to employ Creoles and Indians to do this work, as white men would at once go down with fever and ague, against which the Indians and Creoles were proof. This fish oil was about the first produce ever shipped out of the county, except furs.

The first marriages in this territory, of which there is any record, were two that took place—one at Chicago and the other at Lewistown—on the same day, July 2, 1823, both then in Fulton county. One was the marriage of Thomas Lee Ross and Susan Nye, who were married in Lewistown by Hugh R. Coulter, J. P. The other was the marriage of Alexander Wolcott and Eleanor Kinzie, (doubtless the daughter of the founder of Chicago), at Chicago, by John Hamilton, J. P. Both marriage licenses were issued by Hugh R. Coulter, county clerk, at Lewistown. The bride of Thomas Lee Ross was a niece to Mr. Bogardus above alluded to.

My sister Lucinda was the first white child born in this immense territory above described. She was born in Lewistown Oct. 7, 1821. She became the wife of Judge William Kellogg of Canton, afterwards a member of Congress, and now resides at Ashtabula, Ohio. Her daughter, Mrs. Judge L. W. James, resides in Lewistown.

For two years after the organization of Fulton county the people of Chicago had to come to Lewistown for their marriage licenses, tavern licenses, ferry licenses, etc., and to do all county business. When a couple wanted to get married they would generally postpone the matter until they found another couple of the same mind, or found some one who wanted a tavern license, and then they would send a man down to Lewistown to do both jobs and thus save expense, as it took a man at least two weeks, horseback, to make the trip, and he would have to camp out in the woods most of the nights because there were but few settlers along the route.

It was a great relief to Chicago when Peoria county was organized in 1825, and the county seat located at Peoria. They could then get their tavern and marriage licenses at Peoria and save fifty miles of travel. So after 1825 Peoria took Chicago under its wing, and took a kind of motherly care over the little thing until it got big enough to take care of itself.*

---

* MANKATO, KAS., July 12, 1897.

Editor Democrat:—I have been reading with deep interest the pioneer sketches of Mr. H. L. Ross, especially the last one relating to Dr. Newton. A great deal has been said about his drinking, etc., but no one has told the good story that he was finally converted and baptized while at the home of my grandfather, Joseph Geyer, near Cuba. My grandparents took care of him during his sickness and death. I have in my posession one of his ancient medical books, and also a queer old forceps with which he pulled the teeth of the pioneers of Fulton county.

GRACE GEYER PURDUM.

The editor must also say that Dr. Newton was buried in the old cemetery. About three years ago, in company with the late Dr. Alex. Hull, the editor was shown the spot where Dr. Newton was buried, although the grave is not marked. It was Dr. Hull's purpose to urge the erection of a suitable monument to Fulton county's first physician, but his death probably frustrated that kindly purpose. It seems to us that the physicians of Fulton county may yet desire to perform this grateful act.—Editor Democrat.

CHAPTER IX.

THE WENTWORTHS AND EARLY CHICAGO.—THE KINGSTONS.
—BROTHER LEWIS' VISIT TO CHICAGO.

In early times two families moved from Lewistown to Chicago—one helping to organize the first Methodist church in that city, and the other the first Presbyterian church there.

Elijah Wentworth and family came from Maine and located first at Vandalia, Ill. In 1823 they moved to Fulton county and settled on a piece of land half a mile northeast of Lewistown adjoining my father's farm. They had three sons—Hiram, Elijah and George; and four daughters—Lucy, Eliza, Sophia and Susan. They were Methodists, and helped organize the first Methodist church in Fulton county. They were very industrious people. Mr. W. was a shoemaker, and his sons engaged in farming. The mother and her daughters carried on an extensive business in manufacturing buckskin gloves and mittens and buckeye and straw hats. The buckskins they bought of the Indians, who killed the deer and dressed the hides beautifully. The buckeye timber came from the river bottoms. The men prepared that very tough and elastic timber by working it into splits that were braided into very handsome and useful hats. They very much resembled the Panama hats afterwards so generally worn by gentlemen in hot weather. The straw used in making the straw hats was cut with a sickle or reap-hook about the time the grain began to form, because it would toughen better than at any other time. The straw was bound into sheafs and laid away for future use. These ladies not only supplied the Lewistown market, but sold gloves and hats at Springfield, Peoria and other distant places. In 1827 Mr. Wentworth and family (except Hiram and Eliza, who were married), moved to Chicago. Eliza married a Peoria merchant named Clark, and one of her daughters became the wife of Edward Sayre, Fulton county's famous pioneer circuit clerk. The Wentworths started from Lewistown with two two-horse wagons. In 1842 Mr. Wentworth made a trip back into Fulton county to visit his son Hiram. He stopped over night with my mother, then living in Canton, and there told me the story of his moving to Chicago fifteen years before. He said that on his trip north, after he left Canton they did not see any white people until they reached Peoria; and not one from Peoria to Ottawa; and not one from Ottawa to Chicago. They camped out at night and slept in their wagons. With their flint-lock guns they killed all the game they needed, and with the provisions they carried with them they fared well on their journey. When they arrived at Chicago they found some fifty soldiers at Ft. Dearborn and some forty or fifty wigwams scattered down the Chicago river and some on the lake shore. There were five of six stores or trading posts, and their trade was chiefly with the Indians. There were not (in 1827) more than ten or twelve white families in Chicago. Some of the traders had married squaws and were raising big families of half-breeds. Mr. Wentworth said a great deal of the land in Chicago, along the river and lake, was low and marshy with numberless muskrat houses scattered about. Mr. Wentworth went back about four miles from the lake and located on a fair eighty-acre tract and improved. His daughters here bought buckskins from the Indians and resumed the manufacture of gloves and mittens. The improvement of Chicago was very slow until in 1830, when emigration began at a lively rate. It was about this time that Mr. Wentworth and family helped to organize the first Methodist church in that city.

Perhaps some of the readers of The Democrat may remember an article that appeared in this paper Feb. 7, 1884. It was an extract from the Northwestern Christian Advocate, stating that Mrs. Lucy Walker Wentworth had died in Chicago, aged eighty-four, and that she and her husband were the founders of Methodism in Chicago, and that they had formerly lived in Lewistown. The editor of The Democrat enquired if any of the pioneers remembered the family. I replied at once. It was the same Wentworth family I am now writing about.

I was never able to learn how much the old gentleman got for his eighty-acre farm, now almost in the heart of the city; but he told me that if he had held to it a little longer it would have made him independently rich.

The other family that moved from Lewistown to Chicago, and helped to organize the first Presbyterian church there, were named Kingston. He was an old Scotch Presbyterian. He took an active part in church affairs in Fulton county, and I believe he was a ruling elder in Lewistown. His son John was about my own age. One of his daughters taught in the Sabbath school. Mr. Kingston kept store in a log building that stood on the site of the late Nathan Beadles' fine residence. The cabin was built by my uncle, Thos. Lee Ross, who carried on the hatter's trade in it until he went to the lead mines in 1827, when Mr. Kingston took the store. I think Mr. K. went to Chicago about in 1830. In 1832 he came back to Lewistown to settle up some business and stopped at my father's house. He said he had come from Chicago to Ottawa in a stage, and from there to Havana by a steamboat. He was very enthusiastic about Chicago's future, and told my father that good lots could then be bought there at from $400 to $600 each, and he urged him to go up and make an investment. But father was then building the Havana Hotel and had a large amount of business on hand, but said he would as soon as possible send Lewis to look at the place. Lewis was then in the Black Hawk war. When he was mustered out he went on to Chicago and spent several days looking over the place. When he came home his report was not favorable. He described the land as resembling that about the mouth of Spoon river and around Thompson's lake; he said Chicago river was about like the Spoon river and that it overflowed like the Spoon river; that it was a swampy country, and that his horse had almost mired down as he rode out to Mr. Wentworth's; he also told about the muskrat houses, and said (it was in 1833) that there was not a house in Chicago that compared in size or finish with the Havana Hotel which my father had just completed. I believe it was the largest house in Illinois at that time. I shall have more to say about that hotel in a future letter.

CHAPTER X.

THE HAVANA HOTEL; ITS CONSTRUCTION.—COURT HELD IN BAR-ROOM OF MY HOTEL, WHERE ABRAHAM LINCOLN ATTENDED.—BLOCK HOUSES BUILT.

I will give a short history of the old Havana Hotel which my father built in Havana in the early pioneer times. It will interest the younger generation of today to know something about the hardships and difficulties the old pioneers had to encounter, and with what fortitude and determination they accomplished whatever they undertook to do. It was certainly a very great undertaking to build such a house at that time. There was no pine lumber to be had nearer than Cincinnati, and the few saw-mills that were in the country at that time had been erected on small streams in Fulton county. Therefore most of the sawed lumber used in the hotel was sawed by hand with a whip-saw. When the building was completed it was in all probability the largest building in Illinois and had cost more money than any other one erected at that time in the state. The building of the hotel was commenced late in 1831 and finished in 1833. It combined hotel and store, and both together was eighty feet long by thirty feet in width, with upper and lower porches ten feet wide on each side of the house. The main part of the hotel was four stories high, and the store part two and a half stories. The first story was built of a stone wall twelve inches thick, and the ground floors were laid with stone. The balance of the building was of wood. There were two large chimneys, with three fireplaces opening into one and four into the other. All the lumber, stone and lime used in building the house were brought from Fulton county. The sills, posts, joists and all the other large timbers were cut and hewed in the woods. The stone was taken out of a hill in Liverpool township north of Thompson's lake and carried by boat down the lake and by the Illinois river to Havana. The lime was burned in the same township and hauled by Zenos Herrington to Havana in a truck-wheeled wagon with two yoke of oxen. The truck-wheeled wagon was built without one particle of iron being used in its construction. The wheels and every part were wholly of wood. Mr. Herrington had no need to halloo for the ferry boat when he came to the river at Havana, for the ferryman could hear the creaking of his wagon half a mile away. The timber used in building the hotel was white oak, ash, and black and white walnut. The weatherboarding and shingles were split out of white oak timber and shaved to a proper thickness with a drawing knife. The weatherboarding was four feet long and the shingles twenty-eight inches. The lath was all split out in the woods, and all the doors, window-sashes and mouldings had to be made by hand. The weatherboarding and shingles were made near Lewistown by Jonathan Cadwallader and his sons Isaac and John. They then lived in Lewistown. They were Quakers, and did a good, honest, Quaker job. The carpenter work was done by Moses, Lewis and Alexander Freeman and Isaac and Jesse Benson. The mason work was done by Benjamin Hartland, and the painting by Andrew Maxfield. I mention these names because they were old settlers and many of their descendants are still living there. About twenty-five years after the hotel and store were built the big house was destroyed by fire, and was uninsured.

My father kept the store and ran the hotel up to the time of his death in 1837. My mother and brother Lewis administered on his estate. His stock of goods and other personal property were appraised at a little over $9,000, and the administrator's sale amounted to a little over $10,000. The sale was made on twelve months' credit, the purchaser giving note drawing twelve per cent. interest. After my father's death the store house and hotel were rented out, and the family moved to Canton. In 1840, when I had taken a wife in Canton, I went back to Havana and took charge of the ferry and of the hotel, and ran them for three years. It was during this time that the county of Mason was organized and the county seat located at Havana. There was no court house at that time, and so court was held in the bar-room of my hotel, and some of the other rooms were used for jury-rooms. It was there that such men as Abraham Lincoln, John J. Harris, E. D. Baker, H. M. Wead, W. C. Goudy and John P. Boice attended the courts and took part in the pioneer law suits. I remember at one of the court terms the afterwards famous Gen. Harding had a narrow escape from death. He was very fond of hunting, and went out one morning to try his luck for a deer. At that time they were very plenty along the Illinois river. He did not have to travel far until he saw a deer, and he drew up his gun and fired at it. But instead of killing the deer the breech-pin flew out of his gun and struck him in the face, making a terrible wound. It was several days before he could be taken home, and he carried the scar until the time of his death. Mr. Lincoln never appeared to care very much about hunting and seldom engaged in that sport. His chief amusement and delight was in telling anecdotes and stories. In the role of story-telling I have never known his equal. His power of mimicry was very great. He could perfectly mimic the Dutchman, the Irishman, or the negro. In the evening after court had adjourned a great crowd would gather around Lincoln in the bar-room to listen to Lincoln's stories, and he seemed to enjoy to the utmost the peals of laughter that would fill the house. I have heard men say that they have laughed at some of his stories until they had almost shaken their ribs loose. I heard of cases where men have been suffering for years with some bodily ailment and could get no relief, but who, having gone two or three evenings and listened to Lincoln, had laughed all their ailments away and had become well and hearty men, and had given Lincoln the credit of being their healer.

It was during the time that my father was building the Havana Hotel that he had a 200-acre farm fenced and broken up a half mile east of Havana, the rails having been made on the banks of Spoon river and boated down that river and across the Illinois.

In 1833, during the Black Hawk war, when so many people were leaving the Military Tract for fear of the Indians, he put his whole force of men to work and built a fort, or block house, at Havana, to be a refuge for the white settlers. The effect of this was to stop the ruinous stampede of people away from Fulton county.

I only speak of these things to show what the old pioneers could accomplish under difficulties when they had a mind to work and accomplish something.*

CHAPTER XI.

ARRIVAL OF JUDGE STEPHEN PHELPS AND WILLIAM PROCTOR.—THEIR KINDNESS TO THE INDIANS.—JUDGE PHELPS' SPORTSMANSHIP.

Among the early settlers who came to Fulton county in the old pioneer times there were none who did more to develop all the avenues of prosperity and to exert an influence

---

*Gen. L. F. Ross informs us that three block houses instead of one were built—one on each side of the hotel in Havana, and one on the west bank of the Illinois river and north of Spoon river on the road to Lewistown. Gen. Ross says the people of Fulton county helped to build these houses. The mouth of Spoon river was then directly opposite Havana, and the ferry ran from Havana to the upper side of Spoon river. This large hotel stood on the south side of Market street on the edge of a high bluff overlooking the river. The bluff has been cut down and the site of the hotel is now vacant.

for the good of society than Judge Stephen Phelps and his son-in-law, William Proctor. They came from the state of New York and stopped for a year or two in Sangamon county, and then moved to Fulton county, settling in Lewistown in 1825. Chapman's History of Fulton County says they came in 1827, but it is an error. I have in my possession a record of the fact that cannot be gainsaid. It is the journal book kept by Norman and Ira Scovill when they ran the ferry over the Illinois river at Havana for my father in 1825 and 1826. It was the only ferry on that river between Peoria and Beardstown, and all the earlier pioneers in Fulton county came over the river at Havana. The Scovills kept the ferry on shares, paying my father one-half of all sums collected on ferriage. They kept a very accurate journal, with full particulars of all parties ferried, giving dates, names, articles ferried, etc. So it is that by referring to this ancient journal I can tell the exact date and year when many of the old settlers came to the county. I will copy a few items from this journal to show the reader how it was kept:

1825.
Feb. 18. Judge Phelps, ferriage of 2 horses, and wagon, and 2 footmen..............$ 0.75
Feb. 23. Judge Phelps, 2 wagons, 4 horses, 2 cows and 1 footman.................... 1.37½
July 27. William Proctor, horses, wagons and footman 2.62½

This shows beyond controversy, I think, when Judge Phelps and Mr. Proctor landed in Fulton county. Then I find these items for the same year, 1825: "Feb. 5, Elijah Putman, ferriage, $2.00;" "July 7, William Walters, ferriage, $2.00;" "July 22, Reden Putman, $2.00;" "July 26, Jacob Ellis, $2.00;" "July 26, Levi Ellis, $2.50." And so the record goes on during 1825 and 1826. It would seem to be a thoroughly reliable—perhaps the only correct record of the dates on which so many famed pioneers came to Fulton county.

When Judge Phelps and his family first came to Lewistown they lived in a log house north of the present M. E. church and west of T. F. Stafford's store and residence. The log house was built by John Jewell. They lived there some six or eight months and then moved (in 1825) to the lots now occupied by the Phelps-Proctor store and Mrs. Mary Phelps' residence. When Judge Phelps bought that property there had been erected on it a two-story hewed log house by John Wolcott, who sold the place to him. Judge Phelps added a log kitchen and had the whole building lathed and plastered, and it was the first lathed and plastered house in Lewistown. Judge Phelps also bought a lot opposite on the west side of Main street and there built a hewed log house about 18x20 feet for a store house; but two or three years later they built a frame addition to their store, and then gave the log store-room exclusively for a camping place for the Indians who came long distances to trade with them. Sometimes the Indians came forty or fifty miles with their pack horses laden with deer skins and furs, and they often would remain three or four days to do their trading with the Phelpses, who had opened up the first store in Fulton county. They were very fair and honorable in all their dealings with the Indians and whites, and their trade increased rapidly.

Judge Phelps had five sons and one daughter who were single when they came to Lewistown, his oldest daughter having married William Proctor. The names of his sons were Alexis, Myron, Sumner, William and Charles.

Judge Stephen Phelps was a man about five feet ten inches high, portly built, with light complexion, and weighed about 200 pounds. His son William at fifty years of age resembled his father very much. The judge had at some period of his life received an injury to his back which hindered him very materially in walking, and was obliged, as long as I knew him, to walk quite slowly and with a cane. But aside from that he had excellent health. He was kind and courteous and sometimes inclined to be a little mirthful. His wife was a tall, slender lady of dark complexion, weighing about 120 pounds, and a better or kinder-hearted lady I do not believe ever lived upon the face of the earth. She was good and kind to all, and everybody loved and honored her. I have often heard it said that a poor man's child or an Indian papoose never went from Judge Phelps' door with a hungry stomach as long as his wife lived.

The Phelpses owed a good deal of their success in their Indian trade to the kind and friendly treatment the Indians received at the hands of Judge Phelps and his wife. There were trading posts at Peoria, but the Indians would come from the vicinity of that place all the way to Lewistown to trade their skins and furs to the Phelpses, for they had confidence in them, and was afraid to trust the Peoria traders. The Phelpses erected a press for the purpose of compressing their pelts and skins into small packages, for more convenient shipment to St. Louis. This machine was something after the fashion of a cotton press, but instead of using screws, wooden wedges were employed to compress the pelts. The compressed package would be about 2x3 feet in size and would weigh from 100 to 150 pounds.

The judge's youngest son, Charles, was near my own age, and as boys were rather scarce at that time, we were a great deal together. We both had our shotguns and were both very fond of hunting and fishing; and when Saturday came around and there was no school, we would strike out for a hunt, both of us being about ten years of age. When Judge Phelps came to Lewistown he brought with him a Dearborn carriage and a large brown horse which they called "Prince." The judge was fond of driving, and would often take Charles and myself in his Dearborn and drive us to where we would find good hunting and fishing. One of our favorite resorts was the spot where Spudaway creek empties into Spoon river. There we would always find plenty of fish and game. The judge was also fond of hunting, and would take his gun when he went out, and would often shoot at game while sitting in his carriage as he drove through the woods. His horse was very gentle and would not scare at the firing of the gun. In those times there were a great many pigeons in the country, and the judge delighted very much in killing them. One morning when I was at the judge's house he had just come in from a hunt with his horse and Dearborn, and had brought home fourteen pigeons and told Charles and me that he had killed all of those pigeons with a rifle ball and at one shot, and he wanted us boys to guess how he had done it. After we had made a good many guesses, and had finally given up the riddle, he then told us how the remarkable feat was accomplished.

There are some other things that I would like to mention in regard to the Phelps and Proctor families, but will continue the story in my next letter. I will also give the readers a week in which to guess how Judge Phelps killed fourteen pigeons with one shot of a rifle ball. In my next I will explain the miracle.

CHAPTER XII.

HOW THE FOURTEEN PIGEONS WERE KILLED WITH A RIFLE-BALL AT ONE SHOT.—THE FIRST PIONEER STORES.—METHOD OF SHIPPING CARGO TO ST. LOUIS.—THE FIRST PENITENTIARY IN THE STATE.—CHRISTIAN CHARACTER AND BENEVOLENT DEEDS OF MYRON PHELPS AND WILLIAM PROCTOR.

In my last I promised to tell how it happened that Judge Phelps killed fourteen pigeons with a rifle ball at one shot. It happened as follows: The judge had gone out one morning with his horse Prince and his Dearborn carriage for a ride, and had taken his shotgun with him as was his custom. After firing a few times at squirrels his shot-bag was empty; but he found in his pocket a rifle ball. So he took his knife and cut the ball up into small fragments of lead and loaded his shotgun with them. He soon came to a threshing-floor on my father's farm, where we had been threshing wheat by having the horses trample it out on the ground. A large flock of pigeons had settled down upon the threshing-floor to pick up the grains of wheat that had mingled with the dirt; and when these pigeons rose in a cloud to fly away the judge fired at them on the wing, bringing down fourteen pigeons at one shot with a rifle ball—cut into fragments.

The first year after the Phelpses came to Lewistown they rented twenty acres of my father's farm and put it in corn. Sumner plowed the corn, and my brother Lewis rode the plow-horse, while I rode the plow-horse for my father's hired man in the adjoining field. It is a singular fact that in the first settlement of the county the eastern men had to have a boy to ride the horse when they plowed corn, while the southern men would always drive their plow-horse with a single line.

After the Phelpses had been in business about two years in Lewistown, Alexis and Sumner established a trading-post at Yellow Banks (now Oquawka) on the Mississippi river, and had a large trade with the Indians of Iowa and Illinois.

William Phelps in his youthful days was very fond of the chase. He kept a pack of hounds that were well trained, and during the summer months he would start out in the morning, as soon as it was daylight, with his horse and hounds and a tin horn for a fox-hunt. The deep baying of his dogs and the blare of his horn could in those times be heard for miles around the village. There were a great many wolves, foxes and wildcats in the country, and he would occasionally start up a lynx or a panther. These animals were very annoying to the farmers, as they would kill a great deal of the stock and carry off the poultry, and William and his hounds contributed very materially to their extermination. The first enterprise that William engaged in after leaving home was to set up an Indian trading-post on Grand Island, ten miles below Havana in the Illinois river. After carrying on this trade about one year he was married to Caroline Kelsey and struck out for the wilds of Iowa where he was engaged for many years in trading with the Indians. He was subsequently engaged in steamboating on the Mississippi river for many years.

The next store that was opened in Lewistown was that of Edward Plude, a Frenchman, and Patrick Hart, an Irishman. They built a frame storehouse on the lot where William Proctor lived for many years, on Main street. They kept the store for about two years, and then my father bought their goods and moved them to a store he had built on the Edwin Harris corner, south of the court house. After my father bought their goods, Plude clerked for my father, while Hart clerked for the Phelpses.

A man named Taylor started the next store. He came from Philadelphia. He brought on a large stock of Indian goods and also brought with him from St. Louis two Frenchmen who were accomplished Indian interpreters, as clerks. Mr. Taylor's ambition was to seize upon the splendid Indian trade secured by the Phelpses. He sent his French clerks out among the Indians to secure their trade, but made a great failure of it. The Phelpses had dealt so honorably with the Indians and white people that no power could break the confidence that was reposed in them, and they held their magnificent Indian trade until the Indians were driven out of the country. Mr. Taylor was a very bright and enterprising man, and while he was in Lewistown he was married to Miss Ruth Cadwallader, a daughter of Jonathan Cadwallader, who then lived in Lewistown. She was a grand, noble and beautiful young Quaker lady. I happened to be going to school in Lewistown at the time and boarded with Mr. Taylor.

The Phelpses had a keel boat built for their own trade to St. Louis which was run by Norman Scovill as its captain. I was present at one time when they were loading this boat at Thompson's lake. The cargo consisted of barrels of pork and honey, packages of deerskins and furs, barrels of dried venison, hams, beeswax and tallow, sacks of pecans, hickory nuts, ginseng and feathers, and dry hides. In an ordinary stage of water it took about four days to run a keel boat to St. Louis, by poles, oars and sails, and from twenty to twenty-five days to return. I had gone to St. Louis one time with my father with a drove of horses, and came back with Norman Scovill on his keel boat. The river was quite high, and we had to do a great deal of "cordeling" and "bushwhacking,"* and it took us twenty-five days to come to Havana. I remember that we stopped at Alton as we came up the river, and all hands went up town to see the new penitentiary that had just been built. There were only two prisoners in the penitentiary, so we had the privilege of seeing the first prisoners ever sent to a penitentiary in the State of Illinois. Before that time the penalty for the commission of a crime was whipping on the bare back.

Mr. Proctor came to the county in 1825, some four months after the Phelpses had come, and lived in a house near to where the Phelpses had stopped, just north of present Methodist church. He lived there a short time while building a two-story log house on the hill near the site of his tannery (the site of the present residence of T. B. Harben). He carried on the tan-yard for several years, and then engaged in the mercantile business, and by fair and honorable dealing he soon built up an extensive trade.

There have been but few, if any, of the early settlers of Fulton county that have done as much to advance the true interests and prosperity of the country as Myron Phelps and William Proctor. Whenever a college, church, railroad, or factory, or any public improvement was wanting, they would generally head the list with the largest contribution. When the first railroad was built through Fulton county Myron Phelps gave more for its construction than any other citizen. I happened to be one of the directors and also treasurer of the road for two years while it was being built, and therefore know

---

* This "cordeling" and "bushwhacking" was the use of ropes by which the boat was pulled by men walking along the shore, or by ropes tied to trees by the use of skiffs—the boat being pulled from tree to tree.

the facts that I am stating. Then the grand and noble Christian characters of these men were a blessing not only to the church of which they were honored members, but to the whole community where they lived. I remember some of the circumstances that attended the conversion of Myron Phelps. I was then living in Canton, and Rev. Robert Stewart was pastor of the Presbyterian church at that place. The Methodist brethren had been wonderfully blest in some of the campmeetings they had been holding, so the Rev. Mr. Stewart and the officers of his church borrowed the Methodist camp ground and all its appurtenances, and concluded they would try it. So they sent off to Springfield and got Rev. John Hale, the pastor of the First Presbyterian church of that place, and also sent to Quincy and got the Rev. Dr. David Nelson of that place to come and help run the meeting. They were two of the strongest and most powerful preachers in the state. The campmeeting lasted for eight days, and there were 150 or 200 conversions. A great many Lewistown people attended the campmeeting. My mother had tent on the ground, and I remember that old Dr. Rice and William Proctor were there during the entire eight days, and took a very active part in the meetings. When the meeting closed Mr. Proctor took Dr. Nelson home with him and he held several meetings at Lewistown. The spirit and influence of that campmeeting seemed to pervade all Fulton county. Dr. Nelson visited Myron Phelps at his home, and it was through his mighty influence that he was converted and became a member of the Presbyterian church. I often heard it remarked that when Myron Phelps was converted that "he was converted soul, body, pocketbook and all," for he was always very liberal and benevolent in giving to all worthy objects. I have understood that Myron Phelps was in the habit of giving $1,000 and Mr. Proctor $500 every year for missionary purposes, besides other munificent gifts. I again recall the time when at Vermont a few of us were struggling to build a small church how Mr.

Proctor came to our rescue and gave us $100 to buy the lot on which that Presbyterian church still stands.

These men carried their religion with them in all their business transactions. Their influence was felt for good all through this pioneer country. In the heavenly world alone will be revealed the good they accomplished. I have been informed that Myron Phelps was in the habit of always closing his store during the hour of Wednesday evening prayer meeting so that his hands could attend the meeting, and if there were any customers in the store at the time they were invited to go along. I am also told that he never went to the polls to vote that he did not take off his hat and cast his ballot with as much conscientious solemnity as he would perform any other religious duty.

CHAPTER XIII.

THE BIG SNOW OF 1830-31 AND TERRIBLE SUFFERING THEREFROM.—DESCRIPTION OF INDIAN WIGWAM.—CHIEF RACCOON AND MY "GOOD LUCK."

One of the most remarkable and startling events that ever took place in the early history of Fulton county and Illinois was the big snow that fell in the winter of 1830-'31. Perhaps no event has ever happened in the history of this western country since its settlement by white men that has caused so much suffering among the people and animals as did the "deep snow."

The old settlers will remember many things about it, but another generation has come on the stage of action since then, and they may be interested in the history of that event and some of the circumstances attending that dreadful, long, cold winter.

The snow commenced falling the latter part of December and continued off and on for about a month, and when it ceased falling the snow in the timber, where it did not drift, was about three feet and six inches on the level, and in the prairies along the fences and in the hollows, where it had drifted, it was ten and fifteen feet deep. The snow lay on the ground about three months and during that time the weather was intensely cold. During many days the mercury ran from ten to twenty degrees below zero. Before that time the winters had been so mild and with so little snow that stock seldom had to be fed more than from four to six weeks during the entire winter, and wild hogs kept in fairly good order from off the mast (acorns). During the whole winter the farmers had been in the habit of gathering only what corn they needed to feed their stock in the fore part of the winter, and the consequence was that the greater part of the crop was in the field when the deep snow came. The farmers had made no provisions for such a catastrophe and there was great suffering among the people. A great deal of their stock died, while the wild hogs, deer and other wild animals in the forests were nearly swept out of existence. The Indians came in great numbers from the high lands and settled on the Illinois and Spoon river bottoms. They brought with them their droves of horses and ponies, and kept them from starving by chopping down small trees of soft wood, such as basswood, cottonwood, elm and soft maple. Their ponies would not only browse upon the limbs and bark of the trees, but would frequently eat up the whole tree. So the Indians got their ponies through the winter with very little loss.

The winter of the deep snow was in many ways favorable to the Indians. The snow storm drove great herds of deer from the prairies and hill country to the river bottoms, and the Indians killed great numbers of them. The deep snow was but little impediment to the Indians in travelling, for they had snow shoes with which they could walk or run over the snow as well, almost, as the whites could go over the bare ground. The snow shoe was made by bending a hickory stick in very much the shape of an ox-yoke; the bottom of the bow would be covered with strips of deer skin to be tied firmly onto the ankles and feet. These shoes were about as heavy as heavy boots. When an Indian in snow shoes got after a deer that had to travel in snow three and one-half feet deep, the Indian was pretty sure to get the deer and cut his throat. The snow was also a great advantage to the Indians in hunting the otter, mink and muskrat. These animals would come out of their dens and leave their tracks or trails in the snow, and the Indians could easily track them, when they could be caught. And it was the same with the fox and raccoon; they could be tracked to their holes in the hills or in trees, when the Indians would spear them out of their holes.

I have heard my father say that he had a bigger trade with the Indians than in any winter before or after. I have no doubt that the same was true of the Phelpses.

One of the prominent camping places selected by the Indians during that winter was on Spoon river about two miles below old Waterford. They had there erected some twenty wigwams. The young readers of The Democrat may be interested in learning how these wigwams were built. A common sized wigwam for a family of eight or ten persons would be about 12x16 feet in size. Small saplings would be cut and set firmly in the ground, big ends down, in rows three feet apart, all round the plat (12x16 feet) to be enclosed. Then the limber tops of the poles would be brought together and fastened with hickory wyths or strips of leather. Then small poles would be tied lengthwise to the saplings, making a cross-barred and solid frame. The whole would then be covered with a heavy matting that had been woven by the squaws from the coarse swamp grass yet to be found on the bottom lands. This completed the wigwam, and it had the shape of a hay stack. An opening was left as a door way and this was protected by a blanket. A pit 2x3 feet in size and eight or ten inches deep would be dug in the center under the wigwam for a fire-place, and there was an opening at the top for the smoke to pass through. The Indians were quite comfortable in these wigwams, with their blankets and furs, in the coldest weather. They never used bedsteads, tables or chairs. They usually sat on packages of skins or sacks of feathers. The whole family usually took their meals out of a wooden tray, using knives and wooden spoons, but no forks. In cold weather they kept their fires burning night and day.

Among the Indians that camped at this place was a chief named Osopin (in English, Raccoon). He had traded with my father when he kept store in Lewistown, and also after he started a store in Havana. He would often buy goods on credit, and was always punctual to pay for them at the time agreed upon. My father entered his name on the ledger, "Raccoon Osopin," which was both his English and Indian names. He was a good friend to my father, and brought many Indians to trade with him. My father often made Raccoon handsome presents. I remember that he once brought him from St. Louis a tomahawk with the handle striped off in red, white and blue, with an iron pipe on the hammer part of the tomahawk, there being an opening through the handle, so the chief could use his beautiful tomahawk as a pipe in which to smoke his tobacco. Raccoon was greatly pleased with this princely gift.

I often helped my father in his Havana store while he was trading with the Indians, and so became very well acquainted with Raccoon and his boys. They took quite a liking to me and had often asked me to go to their wigwam and take a hunt with them. My father had brought a small Indian pony for me to ride when I went hunting. So when the deep snow had been sufficiently beaten down into a road between Lewistown and Havana, I started one day with my pony and gun for the Indian camp on Spoon river. When I got there I found that the young Indians had all gone hunting, and only Raccoon was left to take care of the wigwam. While I was warming at the fire he produced a buckskin roll of sinews that had been taken out of the legs of deer. When an Indian kills a deer he always takes the sinews out of its legs to use in place of thread in sewing their moccasins, mittens, etc.; and they also use these sinews about their persons as charms, or for "good luck," as they call it. So Raccoon tied a bit of sinew in the buttonhole of my vest. He said it would insure me good luck, and that I would become a brave hunter. After staying a couple of hours I started back home on my pony. I had not gone over a mile when I saw a large deer standing on the ice in a little lake near the road. He was browsing from bushes, and did not see me. There was a large tree about eighty yards from the deer. I tied my pony to a tree and with my gun in hand crept silently toward the tree, keeping it between me and the deer. Then I rested my gun against the tree, took good aim and fired. The deer fell, but immediately jumped up and commenced to flounder around in the deep snow. I saw that I had only wounded him, and was terribly afraid that he would get away. I never thought of reloading my gun and shooting him again, as I should have done, but left my gun at the tree, and with my knife in my hand ran as fast as I could to the deer. It was jumping around in the deep snow, and I slipped up behind it and cut its ham-strings, which stopped its jumping. It then settled down in the snow, and I got it by the ears and cut its throat. It was soon dead. I little realized the great danger I had encountered in attacking a wounded deer, but found out, after I got older, from talks with old deer hunters, that a wounded deer was the most dangerous animal that runs in the woods. I was then but a little past thirteen years old, and small of my age, and if the deer had turned upon me he would have stamped me to death. The next problem I had to solve was how to get my deer home, for if I left him there the wolves would eat him before morning. I was three miles from home, about north of what is called California Bend in Spoon river. It was about February 1st, and the weather was terribly cold. But I took my pony and gun to where the deer was lying. I took my saddle girth and placed it around the pony's breast instead of under his belly, and with the halter strap hitched the deer to the stirrups. It made a very good harness. I then got on my pony with my gun and started for Havana. It was a hard pull for my little pony to get the deer out of the deep snow, but when we got onto the beaten track it was easy sledding. I crossed the Illinois river on the ice and got home a little after dark. It was the first deer I ever killed, and I was very proud of my success. When Raccoon came in, a few days later, and I told him of my success, he was much pleased; he patted me on the back and said I would be a great hunter. Then he pointed to the bit of sinew he had tied in my button-hole, saying it was the cause of my good luck.

The Pottowatomie Indians that lived about Lewistown and Havana were soon moved to an Indian reservation in Kansas by the government. During Johnson's administration, thirty years later, word was sent to Washington that some of those Indians were in a starving condition. My brother Lewis, then a member of Congress, was appointed with two other members of Congress to go to the reservation to investigate the matter. Arrived there he found a good many Indians he had known in Fulton county, and among them our old friend Raccoon. There was great rejoicing among those Indians when they found out who my brother was, and they had a doleful story to tell him of the hard treatment they had received after they had been driven from their good hunting grounds on Spoon river.

I shall have more to say of these Indians in a future letter.

CHAPTER XIV.

MEETING OF BROTHER LEWIS AND CHIEF RACCOON IN INDIAN RESERVATION.—INDIAN TRAITS.—TRAGEDY IN DEAN'S SETTLEMENT.

In my last letter I spoke of the visit made by a Congressional committee, including my brother Lewis, to the Indian reservation in Kansas, where it was reported that great suffering existed among the Indians. As there were no railroads, these members of Congress had to make the trip on horseback. They passed through many Indian reservations and got all the information they could from the Indians, from their agents, and from missionaries and school teachers who located among them. They found that some of the tribes were in a most deplorable condition and on the verge of starvation. The Pottowatomie Indians that had been driven from the Lewistown and Havana country had been placed upon an Indian reservation in Kansas and were drawing a small annuity from the government, as an alleged compensation for the lands that had been taken from them in Fulton county, but it was not half enough for their support. They had undertaken to farm the land in Kansas, but the locusts, grasshoppers and hot winds of that country had ruined their crops. To make it still worse for them, the government had taken away their guns, so they had to hunt game with their bows and arrows.

As I have said, my brother Lewis found many Indians that he had formerly known at Lewistown and Havana, and who had for years traded with my father and the Phelpses. These Indians were wild with delight to meet him, and could only express their joy by shaking his hands and hugging him. He had there met the old chief, Raccoon, who was delighted to see him. Raccoon inquired about his father and Judge Phelps, and when Lewis told him that they were both dead the tears rolled down the swarthy face of the old chief, and he said, "They were good men to the Indians." The missionaries at the agency told Lewis that Raccoon had been converted and had joined the church with several of his family, and that he took an active part in carrying on the schools and in missionary work among the Indians.

Judge Phelps and my father had always been good friends to the Indians. They believed that it was the safest and best policy to treat them as friends, although they would sometimes lose a little by their stealing, for it was as natural for the Indians to steal as it was for the smoke to go upwards. But all that they would steal amounted to but very little. In the early settlement of the county there came a good many settlers from the southern states, many of whom had had relatives and friends massacred by the Indians of the South, and these southerners as a rule looked upon these Indians as their natural enemy —that they had no rights that a white man was bound to respect. They believed that "the only good Indian was a dead Indian," and they would often get into trouble with them. The hogs of the white men would run in the woods, and the Indian dogs would chase and worry them; and then the white men would shoot their dogs, and then the Indians would shoot their dogs and sometimes their hogs to get even with them. Sometimes a white man would have something stolen from his place, and the Indians would always be accused of the theft; and then the first Indians they could find would be most cruelly whipped with hickory poles, when in all probability the Indians knew nothing about the stealing. The outraged Indians would then go to Judge Phelps or my father and tell them how they had been abused, and would always get their sympathy when they thought they were wrongfully treated. These men would often remonstrate very seriously with these settlers for their inhuman treatment of these Indians.

I can remember some of the circumstances of a tragedy that took place in the southeast part of the county in what was called "Dean's Settlement." Among the settlers there was a man named William Richardson. He was a large, stout man, and was a bitter enemy to the Indians. He would often catch them and cruelly whip them without just cause, and would kill their dogs whenever he came across them. One day when he was out in the woods hunting he came across one of his hogs that had just been killed in the woods. He told some of his neighbors he knew the Indians had killed his hog, and he was going to have his revenge. A day or two later a dead Indian was found propped up, sitting on the dead hog. There were a good many Indians at the time living on Grand Island in the Illinios river, opposite the Dean Settlement, and they were informed about the dead Indian and came and took him away and buried him. They were terribly incensed about the murder and claimed that the Indian was out hunting when he was shot down in cold blood and that he had never killed a hog, and had never done the white people an injury. There was little doubt among the settlers that Richardson had brutally shot down the Indian from ambush and had brought his body and placed it on the hog to strike terror to them; that if they killed hogs their lives would have to pay the penalty. The Indians would have in all probability taken vengeance on Richardson but for another tragedy which soon took place.

Richardson had a neighbor named Bassett who lived about a mile away who believed that Richardson was too friendly with his wife. He went from home one time and came back unexpectedly very early in the morning; and as he came near his home he saw Richardson coming out and starting for his home. Bassett went into his house, took down his rifle, and took a near cut across the woods for Richardson's house, and got ahead of him and secreted himself behind a tree, and as Richardson came along he shot him dead in his tracks.

CHAPTER XV.

CAPTAIN JOHN AND HIS SQUAWS.—THE INDIANS' PARADISE.—INDIAN TRAFFIC IN GINSENG AND WILD POTATOES, AND THEIR EXTERMINATION BY WILD HOGS.

I will give a short sketch of one of the most remarkable Indian families that ever lived in Fulton county. I am sure no other family of Indians ever caused so much gossip and so much bitter denunciation from the female part of the community, both white women and squaws, as did the conduct of an Indian chief called "Captain John." He was a large, fine-looking Indian about six feet, four inches tall, and was one of the most prominent chiefs in the Pottowatomic tribe. It was told by some of the other Indians who had known him before he came to Fulton county that he had taken the side of the British against the Americans in the war of 1812, and that it was while he was amongst the British soldiers that he obtained the name of "Captain John." He and his squaw had learned to speak some words in the English language. The first we knew about them they had their wigwam on Big Creek near the road that ran from Lewistown to Totten's Prairie (now Smithfield). Their wigwam was about three miles northwest of Lewistown close by the dismantled little village of Milton. It appeared from what the Indians told that "Captain John" had at one time became jealous of his squaw, and in his wrath, while under the influence of bad whisky, had bitten off her nose. She wore a buckskin patch over it, and it gave her a most hideous appearance. To add insult to injury, "Captain John" took to himself two young wives. They were handsome young squaws about twenty-two and twenty-four years old, and he took a god deal of pride in dressing them up in the most gay and gorgeous style. No squaws in all that part of the country were able to dress as fine as "Captain John's" young squaws. They had long black hair which they braided and left to hang gracefully over their shoulders, with the ends tied in bows of gay ribbon. They wore large silver earrings, and four or five strands of large glass beads around their necks. Their dresses were of a gay color with a row of silver brooches down the front. Their skirts were of the finest quality of blue cloth. They wore bands of silver clasped on their wrists, and their fingers were decorated with many rings. Their moccasins were ornamented with beads and fine needlework. "Captain John" appeared to be very proud of his young squaws. But the lot of the old squaw was a hard and bitter one. She went poorly dressed, much below the average of other squaws that came to town. "Captain John" and his three squaws were in the habit of coming to town about once every week to trade at Phelps' store, and they always passed by my father's house. "Captain John" always appeared at the head of the procession, a fine and stately figure; next came his two young squaws in all their finery, and the poor old squaw brought up the rear with a package of peltry strapped across her shoulders and bending pitifully under its weight. She was compelled to do all the hard work. The white women and some of the squaws were so indignant at "Captain John" and his two young squaws for the way they treated the old squaw that they would have liked very much to have mobbed all three of them, but "Captain John" was a big chief, and they were afraid of him. But as the country began to settle up with white men the story became current among them that "Captain John" had been identified with the British army, and fought against the Americans in the war of 1812, and also that the British officers had paid a bounty to the Indians for American scalps; and they were disposed to believe that all the money "Captain John" was spending in dressing his young wives so gorgeously had not been obtained by selling deer-skins and furs, but that it had been paid to him for his services against the Americans, and perhaps for some of the scalps of their white brethren. Adding these things to the cruel treatment of the old squaw, of which everybody was cognizant, a very bitter feeling was aroused against him among the men as well as amongst the women. It was very seldom that an Indian had more than one squaw. I have known one or two instances where an Indian had one or two squaws, but never before where they had as many as three. So bitter was the life of this poor old squaw that she often wished that she could leave this cruel world and go to the Indian's happy hunting ground where she would be no longer tormented with rival wives and a cruel husband. The only relief the poor old thing had from her sorrows was to drown them in whisky. She had no trouble to find some person who would let her have whisky, for it was the general impression that the only comfort she ever had was when she was hilariously drunk. In that condition she would tell in broken English the story of her hard lot—what a bad Indian "Captain John" was, what a good squaw she had always been, how "Captain John" had got drunk and bit off her nose, that his two young squaws were no good, that they would not work, and that she had all the work to do, etc., etc.

So it came about that "Captain John" found that it was not safe for him to stay in that part of the country any longer; and he packed his goods on some ponies and with his three squaws moved up to the Rock river country among the Black Hawk tribe. I never heard from "Captain John" and his squaws after that time.

It is probable that there is no other country in the United States in which the Indians so delighted to live and which they were so sorry to leave as the beautiful hunting grounds embraced in the counties of Fulton, Schuyler and Mason. It was a perfect paradise for them. They could find about everything that their hearts could desire, and it was about as good a place for the poor white man as it was for the Indian. The deer roamed through the country by the thousands. It is not an exaggeration to say that I have seen 500 deer in the woods and prairies in a single day. Every other kind of game and fowl was abundant, and the rivers and small streams were full of fish. The bee trees were so numerous that white settlers and Indians could get all the honey they wanted, and there were groves of sugar trees all over the country from which an abundance of maple sugar was made. The wild fruit was equally wonderful, there being no limit to the plums, crabapples, grapes, black and redhaws, gooseberries, blackberries, dewberries and strawberries. Acres upon acres of wild onions could be found in the woods, and wild potatoes in great abundance. Potato creek, south of Spoon river, received its name from the great abundance of wild potatoes that grew on its bank. The hard freezing in the winter did not affect them and they were about as good to eat as Irish potatoes. There was another valuable plant that grew in the woods, called ginseng. The roots resembled very much the parsnips familiar in our gardens. Ginseng grew in the woods in the rich loam, and great quantities of it would be dug and sold to the merchants, who would sack it and send it to St. Louis. It was used for medical purposes and brought a good price. The Indians had a large traffic in digging ginseng and wild potatoes, which they sold to the merchants and settlers. But when the hogs became very numerous in the woods, they soon exterminated both the ginseng and the wild potatoes.

CHAPTER XVI.

APPEARANCE OF THE COUNTRY WHEN EARLY SETTLERS ARRIVED.—EXTENSIVE AND BEAUTIFUL PRAIRIES.—MY EXPERIENCE IN HAULING HAY.—DISCOVERY OF COAL BY MR. GARDINER.—FIRST BANKING ESTABLISHMENT IN FULTON COUNTY.

I have been asked by some of my old friends in Fulton county to tell something about how the country looked when the first settlers arrived in it, about the groves, the prairies, the watercourses and the kinds of wild animals found in the country. So I will endeavor to answer some of these questions.

The face of the country has undergone a wonderful change in appearance, aside from the great improvements that have been made. The beautiful groves of timber then standing unmarred by the woodman's ax have been cleared away; and the handsome prairies, that were then covered with high grass and beautiful flowers, have been broken up, so it is hard to tell which was timber and which was prairie land. There is one thing that has altered the looks of the country very much since it was first settled, and that is the extensive growth of young timber and brush, unknown in pioneer times. Before the county was settled by white people, prairie fires were permitted to sweep through the country every year, and they destroyed what is now called "barrens" and underbrush. The smooth prairies came square up to the distinct groves of large timber. In those days a man traveling through Table Grove, and many of the other groves in the county, could see a deer 500 or 600 yards away in the prairie; but twenty-five or thirty years later a deer could not be seen a distance of fifty yards because of the growth of the brush and young timber. There was no such land in the county as that now called "barrens." The groves were very beautiful before any of the timber had been cut, and before there was any undergrowth. Table Grove was one of the great landmarks of the country. It could be seen from the bluffs of the Illinois river on the east, and from Macomb on the west, and from the north for twenty-five or thirty miles. Travelers across the unbroken and almost pathless prairie were guided in their course by Table Grove and other perspicuous groves.

Many of the streams of water, such as Big Creek, Sugar, Otter, Copperas, Cedar and Buckheart Creek, would run grist and lumber mills about two-thirds of the year. These streams and their valleys, covered by a thick growth of timber and full of wild game, were beautiful beyond words.

The prairies were generally named after the men that first settled upon them. The prairie where Canton stands was called "Barnes' Prairie," for David W. Barnes, who was the first settler there. The prairie west of Cuba was called "Totten's Prairie," in honor of William Totten, who was the first settler. The prairie in Pleasant township was named "Rowland's Prairie," for William and Riley Rowland, the first settlers. The prairie on the Illinois bottom south of Spoon river was called "Gardiner's Prairie." An old Scotch Presbyterian settled there in 1823. He had two sons and three daughters. He was the father of James and Charles Gardiner, whose names are frequently mentioned in Chapman's History of Fulton County. But no allusion has been made to the old father. He was one of the most exemplary Christian men, as well as most enterprising, among the early pioneers. He never failed of holding family worship morning and evening, and would always ask a blessing at the table, and after the meal was through no one was allowed to leave the table until he had returned thanks. Such devotion was remarkable among the early pioneers. He moved from Springfield, and brought with him nursery stock for the famous orchard that for a long time was known all over that country as "Gardiner's Orchard." Gardiner's Prairie extended south from Spoon river about three miles, and from the bluffs to a fringe of timber within half a mile of the Illinois river, also three miles. The land was very rich, but part of it was too wet for cultivation. The prairie that joined Thompson's lake, north of Spoon river, was about two miles square, and with the lake was named for Nathan Thompson. He and his son-in-law, Stephen Meeker, were the first settlers on that prairie. The prairie two miles east of Lewistown was about three miles long and from one to two miles wide, and it was called "Smith's Prairie" after Jeremiah Smith, who first settled there on a place that was afterwards owned by Col. Reuben Simms. It was one of the most beautiful prairies mortal eyes ever beheld. It was covered with what was called blue-stemmed grass, a most excellent grass for hay. It grew from three to four feet high, and afforded hay enough for all the people of Lewistown and the settlers for many miles in all directions. All the people had to do was to cut the hay and haul it home. At that time hay was cut with a scythe and raked together with a wooden hand-rake and pitchfork. Among my recollections was of riding a horse to haul hay on Smith's Prairie. I was a little codger of seven or eight years. We had to haul the hay together for stacking on what was called a brush sled. A small, bushy tree would be cut down and some of the limbs cut off so as to make a sort of flat surface; and the hay would then be piled on top; a horse would be hitched to the contrivance by a chain or rope, and so the hay would be hauled to the place where it was to be stacked. And that was what we called a "brush sled." Many a hot summer day I have rode the old horse to haul hay on the Smith Prairie, where the Rices, W. W. Smith, Samuel Campbell, J. Wertman, W. C. Harrison, the Lawses, Rileys and Chapins now live.

One time the green-head flies attacked my old horse so bad that he ran away. My strength was not sufficient to hold him; after he had run about half a mile I jumped off but did not jump far enough to miss the brush top that he was dragging, so I was caught under the brush sled, and was so badly bruised that I was laid up for repairs for several days. The old horse never stopped running until he got home.

Smith's Prairie was celebrated for the numerous plum and crabapple orchards that grew round its borders. The large red and yellow plums grew there in such abundance that people would come from long distances and haul them away by the wagon-loads, and would preserve them with honey or maple sugar, which were the only sweetening we had in pioneer times. This fruit made a good substitute for domestic fruit. Fulton county was blessed above other sections of the state in its great abundance of sugar-tree groves, which enabled people to make their own sugar.

There is one other thing that will appear very remarkable. When the first settlers came to the county there was no one that appeared to have the remotest idea that there was such a thing as bituminous coal all about them in the earth, or that it had any use. The only people who had lived there were the Indians, and they never used it, and the people would as soon have thought of looking for gold or silver as looking for coal. It was about two years after the first settlement was made that coal was discovered. Meantime blacksmithing was one of the first things needed in the settlement, and a coal pit was built and charcoal burned and used until stone coal was discovered. The first coal found in the county was discovered by old Mr. Gardiner, whom I have referred to as having settled about ten miles south of Lewistown. He was out one day to look for stone to build a fireplace in his log house which he had just erected, and in digging for stone he found the coal bank which was situated at the foot of the bluff east of what is now known as Isabel church. Mr. Gardiner took a load of the coal to Lewistown, and the people were highly delighted to learn that stone coal had been found in the county. The next coal bank that was discovered was on Big Creek about where the Narrow Gauge crosses it three miles north of Lewistown. Another bank was discovered three miles southwest of Lewistown. But the Gardiner bank supplied all the people south of Spoon river and at Havana with all the coal they wanted free of charge. All they had to do was to go and dig and then haul it home. I remember that when I was living in Havana of going with Mr. Eastman Call to the Gardiner bank to dig coal. Mr. Call had just opened a blacksmith shop at Havana, which was before he opened a shop at Lewistown. It took but a short time to fill our wagon with coal. So I could have it to tell that I had dug coal out of the first coal bank that was ever opened in Fulton county.

May I also be permitted modestly to recall the fact that I opened the first banking establishment in Fulton county. It was a branch of a Jacksonville state bank, and was located in the town of Vermont in 1859, and was called the "Fulton Bank." The bank bills were issued and printed at Jacksonville, Illinois. I was appointed agent, and had the entire supervision and control of it. I can say that no depositor or patron of that bank ever lost a dollar through his dealings with it. So I have had the honor of digging coal out of the first bank ever discovered in Fulton county, and also of operating the first bank ever opened in Fulton county, and one occupation was as honorable as the other.

CHAPTER XVII.

JOHN COLEMAN, A REMARKABLE PIONEER.—LITTLE PIKE'S FIRST RIDE.

Amongst the early pioneers of Fulton county there was one man whose name the historians of the county have failed to mention, who, to my mind, was one of the most enterprising men in the county, and for the first fifteen or twenty years of the county's settlement did more to develop and improve its resources than any other citizen.

His name was *John Coleman*. He moved from New Jersey to Fulton county in 1827, coming the entire distance in two and four-horse wagons. He bought a half-section (320 acres) of land a half mile north of the then hamlet of Canton. He was a large man, weighing some 200 pounds, and his wife was a large woman. They had five sons and three daughters. They were all industrious, good workers, and in a few years they had in cultivation the largest and best farm in Fulton county. They planted out a good orchard, and located on the farm a blacksmith shop and a horse-mill, and also a dairy for the manufacture of butter and cheese. While living in New Jersey Mr. Coleman had carried on the business of manufacturing axes, and when he got his shop started he continued the business of making axes, and they were probably the first axes that were manufactured in the state. His axes were all stamped with the name "J. Coleman," and were warranted that if an ax broke with proper usage he'd either mend it or replace it with a new one. He found a good sale for them. It was a good thing for the people that such a man had settled among them. He also brought with him a stock of dry goods, which were the first goods brought to the vicinity of Canton, and the next stock brought to the county after the Phelpses had opened a store at Lewistown.

There were some little circumstances that happened about the time that the Coleman family came to the county that I will mention. They crossed the Illinois river at Havana and came up through Lewistown and camped near my father's house, who then lived north of Lewistown, where Major Walker now lives. Mr. Coleman came to the house to buy some corn and hay to feed their horses, and my father enquired where they came from, and he replied from New Jersey; and when my mother learned that they had come from New Jersey, she became interested in them, as that was her native state, having been born and raised there. And she invited him to bring his wife and stay in the house over night. He remarked that they had not slept inside of a house since they left New Jersey; that they camped out and slept in their wagons. But they came over and spent the evening in talking over New Jersey with my mother, and stayed all night. The next morning Mr. Coleman, in looking over my father's stock of cattle, took quite a liking to a large yoke of oxen that he had and proposed buying them. My father told him he could have them for $40. He said he would take them if he could pay for them in goods; that he had brought along a stock of goods; that they were packed away in his wagons, and that he did not want to open them until he got some buildings put up, which he thought would take him five or six weeks. So my father let him have the oxen, agreeing to trade them out after he got his store opened. So in about six or seven weeks my mother concluded that she would go up and trade out the price of the oxen, and as my father was engaged at the time, and could not go with her, he got a young man named Silas Chase, a son of old Esq. Stephen Chase who lived in Lewistown, to go with her and drive the horse and buggy. They got along all right until they got to the Big Creek hill, which was about a half mile long. The timber all the way down the hill had stood densely thick, and a narrow road had been cut out between the trees just wide enough for a wagon to pass. As there were but few people at that time to do road work, the trees had been cut to make the roadway and the stumps left standing in the road. My mother had taken my youngest brother, Pike, along with her. He was between two and three years old. Just as they started down the hill some of the harness broke and let the single-tree strike the legs of the horse, which frightened him terribly, and he ran with all the speed that was in him down the hill, my mother expecting every moment that the buggy would strike a stump or a tree and dash them all to the earth. When they had got about half way down the hill she gathered little Pike and lifted him over the hind end of the buggy, holding him by one arm until his feet touched the ground, and then dropped him, the horse running all the way down the hill as hard as he could tear. The young man could not hold him, but endeavored to guide him so as to miss the stumps and trees. When they got to the foot of the hill the horse plunged across Big Creek just below Ellis' mill dam. The water was about three feet deep, which checked the speed of the horse, and as he ascended the opposite bank the driver stopped him. Young Chase then got out, tied up the broken harness, and then turned around and drove across the creek to go and hunt up the boy. They met him coming toddling along down the hill, and all right. That was his first ride, and he probably thought that that was the way the thing had to be done. They took him in and crossed the creek again and started on their way to Coleman's.

When they got there they found that he had put up two log houses, with a hall running between them, with a door opening from the hall into each of the houses. One of the houses was intended for a store and a bedroom, and the other for a dwelling. They had not had time to put up any counters and shelves, but had erected in the storeroom three bedsteads, and the goods had been unloaded from the wagons and piled under the beds. They had one son called Jerry, who was lame, but could assist in the store; and when my mother would call for an article of goods Jerry would be sent under the bed to hunt it up. She said that she thought that Jerry had been sent under the beds at least twenty times for goods by the time she got done trading.

A short time after the Coleman family came to the county their oldest daughter, Joanna, was united in marriage to Thomas Wolf, and they settled about four miles east of Canton. They were all industrious, good farmers, and made number one good citizens.

There were some things rather remarkable about John Coleman in regard to his financial operations. At that time there were no such institutions in the county as banks or banking houses, and Mr. Coleman answered very well the need of such an institution, for if a man came into the county with money that he did not want to use, Mr. Coleman would always take it of him if he could get it at five or six per cent interest; and if another man came along that wanted to borrow some money, Mr. Coleman always accommodated him if he would pay ten to twelve per cent interest, and could give the requisite security. There was no doubt but that he saved many a man from having his land sold for taxes, or property sold for debt, by loaning him money. So he was certainly a benefactor to the community in which he lived. It was well known that he handled a good deal of money, and the great query was where he kept it, for at that time there was no such thing in existence as an iron safe to keep money in. But it was told by some that had done business with him that he had made an iron box, as he was a blacksmith, and kept his money in that, and had it secreted under his bedroom floor; and when he wanted to have access to his money, all that he had to do was to pull up a puncheon of the floor and take out the iron box.

Mr. Coleman was regarded by his neighbors as a very honorable and just man in all of his dealings, and his word was considered as good as his bond.

But there came a time when he had to pass through one of the most tragical and awful ordeals that had ever happened to him during all of his long and honorable and useful life. It was on the occasion of what was called "Westerfield's Defeat," a terrible Indian scare that took place at Canton during the Blackhawk War. The cause of the terrible Indian fight, and the stampede of the people that followed it, and the prominent part that Mr. Coleman took in the affair, I will have to leave for my next letter.

CHAPTER XVIII.

THE WESTERFIELD INDIAN SCARE.—MEMORABLE CYCLONE OF 1835.—UPRISING OF CANTON'S WOMEN AGAINST THE SALOONS OF THAT VILLAGE.

The pioneer hamlet of Canton passed through three dreadful ordeals of horror and excitement:

The first was "Westerfield's Defeat" in March, 1832, a dreadful Indian scare.

The second was the memorable cyclone of June 18, 1835, in which five Canton people were killed, many houses blown to pieces, and goods and furniture scattered over the prairies and forests even into Mason county.

The third great event was the uprising of Canton's women against the saloons of that village in which men stood aghast while 100 valiant mothers, wives and sisters gutted the saloons and routed the whisky sellers.

But I have promised to tell the story of John Coleman's connection with Westerfield's defeat, as I witnessed part of the events. There were many reasons in 1832 why the people of Fulton county should be in apprehension of a raid and general massacre by Black Hawk and his great army of Indians. This county for ages had been their home. Here were their favorite hunting grounds and loved sugar groves unsurpassed on the whole continent. Here were the graves of their sires. The Indians venerated their dead as white people do not. They had holy burial places at Duncan's, Walters' graveyard (where there are Indian graves to this day), at Mount Pleasant, and at hundreds of spots along the Spoon and Illinois rivers and all over the great woods of Fulton county. These Indians knew their lands had been wrongfully taken from them, and that the venerated graves of their dead had been ruthlessly plowed and desecrated. They had only been driven out of the county about two years before. The great chief Black Hawk was at this time making his last heroic stand on Rock river. The memorable battle of "Stillman's Defeat" had just been fought with victory to the Indians, and among the dead were Bird Ellis, Tyus Childs, John Walters and Joseph Farris of Fulton county. Many others were wounded. Among these was Major Samuel Hackelton, who lived on Spoon river, four miles south of Lewistown, a few rods west of the spot where the C. B. & Q. bridge now spans that stream. He had a single combat in that fight with a chief, both armed with knives. The chief was killed, but Hackelton received serious wounds that disabled him for a long time. This battle was followed by dreadful Indian massacres in the Rock river country in which men and women were killed and scalped and little children chopped to pieces by the savages.

Then between Canton and Rock river was 100 miles of wilderness. The Indians could come unheralded to the cabins of the settlers. All these things were known to the pioneers, and there was general apprehension and alarm in the spring of 1832. During March scouts were kept on the outskirts of the settlement to give warning if bands of Indians should appear. There was such gloom and alarm that many people loaded their household goods and moved over the Illinois river into Sangamon county, where the settlements were larger, and where they would be safe. Among these were the wife and younger members of the family of John Coleman. Meantime the people of Canton erected a fort or block-house to go into if necessary.

One day Peter Westerfield, an old elder of the Presbyterian church of Canton, and a Frenchman, Charles Shane, went on an independent scouting expedition of their own. Some ten miles northwest of Canton they came upon a trail running through the grass which they were sure had been made by traveling Indians. In fact it was the path made the day before by a band of soldiers en route from Beardstown to join their company on Rock river. Westerfield and Shane immediately hurried back to Canton to report their important and alarming discovery. As they neared Canton they heard shooting and shouts of a party of fool young hunters who had treed a lot of game. Of course they assumed that it was Indians massacreing white families who lived just there. They rode furiously into the hamlet of Canton, yelling wildly at every cabin they passed, "The Indians are on us! The Indians are on us!" There was an immediate panic which no words will describe. People hastily gathered their wives and little ones and rushed either to Canton or to the brush, hoping to escape the scalping knives that seemed hanging over them. In Canton there was the wildest alarm. Mr. Westerfield had the confidence of the people. They believed his report implicitly. The more timid started a-foot and by every means of conveyance toward Havana and Sangamon county. Others gathered at the Canton fort to make the best defense they could. The story of heroism and helplessness from fright would fill many columns.

John Coleman and his son Jerry were at their store and residence a half-mile north of Canton. They quickly started to join Mrs. Coleman and children at Havana, and as they passed along south through the Wilcoxen neighborhood they gave the alarm at every cabin they passed. These people in turn gave the alarm to their neighbors in what is now Buckheart, Liverpool and Waterford townships, as the road from Canton to Havana passed four or five miles east of Lewistown.

Mr. Coleman and his son got to the ferry at Havana about 4 o'clock in the afternoon. My father was keeping the ferry at that time, and had two boats—one large one for heavy teams, and a smaller one for horsemen and buggies. As a lad I was then steersman for the smaller boat, and was an eye-witness to the stirring events of that time in Havana. We heard the frantic yells of Mr. Coleman through the dense timber half-a-mile away from the ferry. As he came nearer we could hear "Indians!" "Murder!" When they got to the boat Mr. Coleman told us of the Indian raid at Canton, of the probable horrid massacre of many families, and that the people were coming to the river in swarms, and that we had better have both boats ready at once, as we would have all we could do to ferry them over. He was entirely correct, for we had only landed them on the Havana side when we again heard hallooing on 'the west side of the river, and the people poured in upon us in such a flood that both boats were kept busy until 11 o'clock at night. The people came a-foot, on horse-back and in all imaginable pioneer conveyances. As many as three of four members of a family would come riding on one horse. There was but one block-house in Havana at that time, and many of these people went right on into the Springfield country.

After the people had all been ferried over the river there were two men who determined to go back to the Canton country and see just what the situation was, and at Canton they learned that it was all a mistake, and that there had not been an Indian within maybe 100 miles of the settlement. So they hurried back to Havana to tell the good news, and the people with unbounded joy began at once to return to their homes. Mr. Coleman and his family had gone on to the Springfield country. But in a few days they returned and were again ferried over into the Fulton county country and returned to their Canton home and store in a much pleasanter frame of mind than when they so suddenly left. But Mr. Coleman was not feeling very amiable toward his neighbor, Mr. Westerfield. But there is no doubt that the old elder was just as honest and sincere in warning his neighbors to flee from Black Hawk's tomahawk and scalping knife as when he was leading a prayer-meeting in the Canton Presbyterian church.

But it was the greatest Indian scare that ever was known in that country.

CHAPTER XIX.

PIONEER HANGINGS.—EARLY LAWYERS.

In all the seventy-five years of Fulton county's history there has never been a legal execution within its limits. In that time there have been scores of murders, many of them meriting the death penalty, but owing to the tricks of lawyers and the weakness of juries, these criminals have all escaped serious punishment.

However, I beg permission in this letter to discuss some of the pioneer hangings that I have witnessed, although it is not a very pleasant subject to write about. But there are valuable lessons connected with these tragedies that will not be lost upon the readers of The Fulton Democrat.

The first execution that I ever witnessed was that of a father and his son who were hung in Rushville, Illinois, in June, 1835. They were Elias McFadden and son David, who lived a mile south of Macomb. The sheriff came one day with an execution to levy on a crib of corn, and got a farmer named John Wilson, a quiet and much respected citizen of the neighborhood, to go with him with his horses and wagon to haul the corn away. When the two men arrived at McFadden's farm the older McFadden in great heat struck the horses with a stick and ordered them to leave the place. But they persisted in levying on the corn, when young McFadden fired from their cabin window and shot John Wilson so that he died within a couple of days. The McFaddens were arrested, but took a change of venue to Schuyler county. They were tried before Judge R. M. Young and prosecuted by Cyrus Walker, prosecuting attorney for that district. The two men were convicted of murder and sentenced to be hung. Notice was given in the newspapers that the execution would be public, and hundreds of people from Fulton, McDonough and Schuyler counties went to see the double hanging.

I was then living at Havana, and with another young

man started to see the execution. On the road we came up with Hugh Lamaster, Nathan Beadles and Robert Gamble, all from Lewistown on their way to Rushville. Mr. Lamaster invited us to stop over night with their party at the home of one of his uncles, about three miles north of Rushville. Here we found a Christian and hospitable home in which no pay would be taken for our entertainment. The next day was the time of the execution, and we found 1000 to 1200 people gathered about the jail to see the prisoners as they were to march to their death. About twenty minutes before they were taken out, a couple of two-horse wagons were driven up to the jail, in each of which was a coffin in plain view. The prisoners were brought from the upper portion of the jail down a flight of stairs on the outside. They were both tall men, and were dressed in white shrouds, with white caps on their heads. They made a very ghostly appearance as they walked down the long stairs and climbed into the wagons and took their seats on the top of their coffins.

I should here remind the readers that when a person was buried they were dressed in white cambric shrouds, similar to those the prisoners wore, which added so much to their horrible appearance. It was not until about in 1845 that the people commenced to bury their friends in their wearing apparel.

The distance from the jail to the place of execution was about a mile, and a long procession was formed, some in wagons, some on horseback, and others a-foot. One of the strangest things about this event was the fact that the wife and mother of the two men was in the procession to go and see husband and son executed. The place of execution was a hollow between two hills which afforded the people a good view of the hanging. It was estimated that from 2,000 to 3,000 people were present. The men both testified that they had both experienced religion while confined in the jail and had received forgiveness for their awful crime. They talked for a few moments, then shook hands with some of their friends, then shook hands with each other, and then embraced and kissed each other, and then the white caps were drawn over their faces and the trap was sprung. As they were launched into eternity the old lady, the wife of one and mother of the other, was only a few rods away gazing intently upon the scene. As the drop fell with her beloved ones dangling at the end of the ropes, she gave one awful scream of anguish and terror and then all was still. After they had hung about fifteen minutes they were taken down and laid in their coffins. It was all so tragical and dreadful to behold that it haunted my young mind by night and by day for many months.

The next hanging that I had an opportunity of seeing was that of Peter McCue, who hung himself in his hatter shop in Lewistown in about 1843. I happened to be in town that day. (His shop was on the spot where the Walter Belless building is now going up.) I was riding down Main street and observed a great crowd of men and boys peeping through the windows to see the body. I got off of my horse and took a peep at him myself. He had fastened a cord to a joist in his hatter shop, and was hanging with his toes just touching the floor. The only person that I can recall, now living, who was present was Maj. Newton Walker. I knew Peter McCue very well, while he was carrying on the hatter's trade, for about nine years. He was single, about thirty-five years of age, an Irishman by birth and a Catholic in religion. He learned his trade in the old country and was a very good and successful hatter. When he put an end to his life he was in the habit of going to St. Louis once a year. His friends used to say it was for the purpose of confessing his sins to a priest. The last time he started on this annual trip he went as far as Havana, and while waiting for a steamboat the Illinois river froze up and he had to return to Lewistown. His friends observed that he was melancholy after his return home, but did not dream that it was a serious matter. It was inferred that his failure to see the priest had something to do with his suicide. I remember that Peter one time made a fur hat for my father for $8.50, and it was well worth the money, for it was one of the most beautiful hats I have ever seen. My father had only worn it three or four times before his death, and my mother subsequently gave it to the Rev. Dr. David Nelson, a Presbyterian minister, who was conducting a camp meeting near Canton, in the fall of 1838, when some 150 or 200 people were converted and joined the church. I have had occasion once before to speak of Dr. Nelson, and will only add that he was one of the early pioneer Presbyterian ministers who traveled through the country between the Mississippi and Illinois rivers and organized very many churches and Sabbath schools.

A year after Peter McCue went to Lewistown I also went there to attend school, and for a long time boarded with Peter with the family of W. C. Osborn. So we were a good deal together. He was kind and friendly disposed, and I had come to like him very much, and was very sad indeed to see the poor fellow hanging dead in his own shop.

Mr. W. C. Osborn, the man we boarded with, was the second lawyer that settled in Fulton county. Hugh R. Coulter was the first lawyer, and William Elliott the third. At that time Mr. Osborn owned the entire block west of the public square in Lewistown, and his dwelling house stood on the south side of the block. He was one of the well-known pioneers of that time.

CHAPTER XX.

SUICIDE OF EDWARD STAPLEFORD AND ITS AWFUL CONSEQUENCE.

The suicide of Edward Stapleford in the town of Vermont, about 1857, had some unusual features. He was a native of Maryland, had run a store in Beardstown, Illinois, and came to Vermont and opened a store in about

1845. He was a shrewd business man and soon had worked up quite a trade. He had frequently engaged in speculations in pork and wheat and anything in which money could be made. Generally he was very successful.

In those time we had no railways, and the only way ot shipping products to market was by steamboats on the Illinois river to St. Louis. We had no telegraphic communications with the world, and but one mail a week; so the most direct way of getting commercial news was from newspapers brought up on steamboats from St. Louis. During the progress of the Crimean war in 1854-'55 the price ot pork and wheat went up to a very much higher price than it had been for many years, and many country merchants in Illinois were ripe for speculation, and Mr. Stapleford was one of the most ambitious merchants among them.

One Saturday evening he succeeded in getting a newspaper direct from St. Louis, and it brought the news that wheat and pork had taken a wonderful rise in price. It was later news than any of the other merchants had been able to get; so he started out early Sunday morning to scour the country and buy up all the wheat and pork he could find. He was afraid to wait until Monday lest the other merchants should also find out the good news and get ahead of him.

I was also keeping store in Vermont at that time, and our stores were close together. The next morning he stopped at my store as he was passing. He was in his happiest mood. It was his trait to be happy when he was making money, but very gloomy if trade was against him.

"Good morning," was Mr. Stapleford's salutation, "where do you suppose I was yesterday?"

I replied that I supposed he was with his family at church.

He then told me of his having contracted with a good many farmers for their pork and wheat. Apparently it was a master stroke.

Mr. Stapleford rushed business with all his might to get his produce en route to St. Louis before the river should freeze; but, alas! just as he was ready to load his pork and wheat on a steamboat cold weather set in, the river was frozen solid, and his stuff laid at the warehouse until the first of April. Then the war had ended, and produce had gone down one-half in price. Of course he was in debt to the St. Louis merchants, and when his produce arrived they were on hand to secure the last dollar due them, and it left him almost nothing to pay the farmers who had sold him their produce on credit.

When he came home it was noised abroad that he had lost big money on his venture. The farmers were in great need of their money to pay their taxes and other pressing debts. So these farmers gathered in crowds and demanded their money, sometimes in no very gentle tones. Mr. Stapleford was very proud and haughty, and these assaults annoyed and angered him tremendously.

One day he went to dinner as usual and ate a hearty meal; nothing unusual appeared in his manner. But as he started out he saw five or six of his creditors lining the street and awaiting his appearance, presumably to renew their appeals for the money due them. He turned round and started for his back door, remarking to his wife:

"I guess I'll fool those fellows."

He went out at the back door, Mrs. S. naturally supposing he had gone to the store by a back way to avoid his creditors.

But a half-hour later he was found hanging by a cord in his barn, and dead. He had "fooled those fellows" by committing suicide! The alarm was given, and great crowds visited the barn to see the grewsome spectacle.

About eight months after Mr. Stapleford moved to Vermont he had married one of the handsomest and most amiable and popular young ladies of the town. She belonged to one of the best families of the place, and was connected with some of the best families of Cincinnati. He was fifteen years her senior, but the marriage was understood to have been a happy one. They had several children, and they were bright and beautiful. His death was such a shock to his devoted wife that she became insane. Her parents cared for her as long as they lived, and after their death she was in the care of Cincinnati relatives. Forty long years this poor wife was a care to those who loved her.

It is strange that any mortal should thus desert such a wife and family by the suicide route.

CHAPTER XXI.

THE PIONEER DOCTOR AND HIS METHODS OF TREATMENT.—THE INDIAN DOCTOR.—HOW HE CURED ME.

In looking backward over the seventy-five years of my past life I am struck with wonder and amazement at the improvements in art, science and literature. The wonder is, what will the next seventy-five years develop?

I shall discuss the advancement made in two of the professions, medicine and teaching. In this paper I will describe the pioneer doctor.

In early times in Fulton county there was no such thing as a drug store. The merchants kept a supply of medicines in stock among their dry goods and groceries. The doctors never gave prescriptions, but carried their medicines around in medicine bags and dosed it out to their patients.

When a doctor was called to see a patient the first thing he did was to examine his tongue, then feel of the pulse at the wrist; then he would have the sick one set up in a chair to be bled. The sleeve of one arm would be rolled up to the shoulder, and the arm extended out to full length, and the hand grasped around the handle of a broom-stick to hold the arm steady and in proper position. A cord would then be tied tightly around the arm half way between the elbow and shoulder, and then the patient was stabbed in a blood vessel of the arm. At first a thumb-lance was used, but the spring-lance came in as a great improvement. They usually took from a pint to a quart of blood, dependent upon the age and size of the sick one. After the bleeding the patient would be given an emetic, and after he had been thoroughly vomited he would be given a dose of calomel and jalop, and then a walloping dose of castor oil. After all those horrors the patient would be taken through a course of blistering. A blister 6x10 inches would be placed upon the breast, with smaller ones on the arms and legs; if the patient was very sick a portion of the hair would be shaved off the head and one of those horrible blisters applied to the head.

The doctors made their own blister-plasters. They carried in their medicine bags a package of Spanish flies, a small cake of tallow and some pieces of canvas. The tallow would be carefully spread over the canvas, the Spanish flies sprinkled over it and pulverized with a caseknife. These flies were large and yellow, resembling yellow wasps. The plasters would be left on from six to eight hours, causing terrible pain. They would then be removed and the blister dressed with cabbage leaves, or a bit of tallowed muslin. Sometimes the blisters would be drawn so deep that it would be two weeks before they would heal; and during the time a white substance would appear in the wound which was called "proud flesh," and it was removed by sprinkling over it powdered roasted alum, this also causing great agony.

One marvelous thing the common people could not understand was that after the patient had gone through with all this bleeding, vomiting, purging and blistering, and been reduced to the very last extremity, he was not allowed by the doctor to take any nourishing food—nothing better than a little thin gruel, a little chicken broth, or a little toast and tea; and while the poor creature, tortured with a burning thirst, might be screaming for water, he was not allowed to have one cool drop, but might have a little warm tea or slippery-elm tea water.

If under this treatment the patient was fortunate enough to get well, the doctor would claim for himself a vast amount of credit for his skill that brought him from the verge of the grave; but if the poor creature died, it was laid to the decree of Providence.

In the early days we had no dentists, and the regular doctors did all the tooth-pulling. They carried an instrument called a tooth-drawer, or "pullikens," shaped like a gimlet, but with a loose hook that was caught around the tooth, and then a twist of the handle brought out the tooth —sometimes. The price for pulling a tooth was 25 cents.

It was three and a half years after the county was first settled by white people before we had a regular doctor. But we found here an Indian doctor who was practicing in Indian families, of whom I will have more to say.

We also found residing near Waterford Dr. W. T. Davison, but he was a hermit and refused to practice or have anything to do with white people; and when they commenced to settle around him he loaded his goods into a canoe and left the county.

The readers will remember Mrs. Jacob Ninan, who once mounted a fleet horse and started for Springfield, 1821. She followed midwifery, and usually with good success. For three years she was present at about all the births in Lewistown and vicinity. But when she was called to attend my aunt, Mrs. Hugh R. Coulter, the child did well, but the mother did not do well, and Mrs. Ninan did not appear to know how to treat her. The Indian doctor was called in consultation, but he told Mr. Coulter his wife would die and he did not wish to prescribe for fear he would be blamed; but intimated that if he had been called at first all would have been well.

Then came a ride for life. My Uncle Thomas Ross at once mounted a fleet horse and started for Springfield, fifty-eight miles distant, for the doctor nearest to Lewistown. He never stopped his wild ride for life, through 116 miles of wild pioneer woods, until he had the doctor at her bedside. The doctor stayed with her twenty-four hours, and then went home. He was eminent in his profession, but could not save her life. She died in two days. Her babe grew to be a fine boy. Mr. Coulter subsequently married a Miss Bushnell, who was killed by a runaway team at Galena, Ill.

My Aunt Maria Coulter was the first person buried in the present cemetery north of Lewistown. All those who had previously died in the village and vicinity were buried in the first graveyard in East Lewistown (the site of the little East Primary schoolhouse). Two of the pall-bearers who attended my aunt's funeral were the late Myron Phelps and John Johnson, then proprietor of Waterford. Some fifteen persons had been buried in the little east cemetery. Some of the bodies were moved to the present cemetery, and others remain there to this day.

The Indian doctor I have referred to practiced medicine in a different manner from white doctors. He was one of the first Indians we got acquainted with in 1821. He was about fifty years old, and could speak a little English. He was very friendly with the white people and soon gained their confidence and friendship. The Indians regarded him as a very great man and had all confidence in him as a doctor. He lived at a small Indian village on the bank of Big Creek, three miles northwest of Lewistown, near the site of Milton. He carried his medicines in a leathern pouch by his side, and rode a fine-looking black pony. He practiced among the Indian families, and often attended the whites, generally giving good satisfaction. His medicines consisted of herbs, barks, root extracts and various oils from beasts, birds and reptiles. Rattlesnake oil was a favorite remedy. Another treatment was to sweat or steam his patient. He would dig a hole 10x10 inches square in a wigwam, get it aglow with live coals, and over this he would place his patient covered with blankets until there was profuse perspiration; in some cases he used steam from a vessel over the coals. The Indian doctor was often in Lewistown, and sometimes went even to Havana to see the sick. Once while we lived at Havana I had taken a serious cold, and father called this Indian doctor, who happened to be there. He gave me some fine powdered substance to snuff up my nose; it set me to sneezing so dreadfully that my parents were alarmed, but the doctor assured them that I was in no danger. The sneezing soon ceased. He next took some herbs and barks from his pouch, made a poultice of them, bound it about my forehead, and next day I was all right.

CHAPTER XXII.

PIONEER SCHOOLS.—FIRST STEEL PENS.—HOW SOME YOUNG LADIES WERE PUNISHED FOR DISOBEYING RULES.—FIRST SCHOOLHOUSE AND ITS CONSTRUCTION.

A history of how the public schools were conducted in the early settlement of Fulton county may be interesting to some of the readers of The Democrat; so I will give a little of my experience and observation in regard to some of them.

For several years after the first settlement of the county there were no public school funds to pay the teachers, and when a school was needed in a town or neighborhood the teacher would go around amongst the patrons of the school with a subscription paper to see how many scholars could be obtained, and if enough could be obtained to justify him in teaching, he would take the school. The term that the schools were taught was three months, and the tuition was from $1.50 to $2.00 per quarter; and if the patrons were satisfied with the teacher they would engage him for another term, but not for more than three months at a time. The branches taught were reading, spelling, writing, arithmetic, geography and grammar. The school would be graded into first, second and third classes.

In opening the school in the morning the first class was required to read a chapter in the New Testament, and, if the chapter was a short one, they would read two chapters, each scholar reading one verse. The teacher would usually consume about half an hour each forenoon in making and repairing pens and setting copies for those that were learning to write. At that time there was no such thing in that part of the country as gold or steel pens, and all the pens used for writing were made from quills plucked from the wings of a turkey or a goose. The first steel pens introduced was about the year 1831. I remember that in 1831 my father went to St. Louis and laid in a stock of goods, and among his purchases were a half dozen cards of steel pens. They came fastened on cards, a dozen on a card. That was as many as any merchant thought it prudent to buy at one time. The use of them was strongly disapproved of by the teachers. They would tell the scholars that they would never become good writers if they learned to write with a steel pen. The price they sold at when they first came in use was $12\frac{1}{2}$ cents a pen. The steel pens at first used were much coarser and heavier than the pens now used, and a very great improvement has been made in them since they first came in use.

It was the custom in those times that when a teacher took a school to make a statement to his scholars of the rules and regulations by which the school was to be governed; and if any of the scholars disobeyed those orders and regulations they were to be punished, whether male or female; and it made no difference how old, or how young, or how large, or how small, they would all come under the same rule; and their rules were like the laws of the Medes and Persians—were unalterable. They had two modes of punishment. One was to be whipped, and the other to stand upon a bench to be gazed at by the whole school until the teacher ordered them to come down.

I will relate some of the circumstances at a time when the school was taught in the old log court house in Lewistown. The schoolteacher was an old Englishman by the name of John Elliott. He had only been a short time from the old country when he came to Lewistown and took the school. He was low in stature, but very fleshy and corpulent, and a fair specimen of a genuine " John Bull." One of the rules of his school was that if any scholar should absent himself from school for fifteen minutes after school was taken up he was to be punished, unless a satisfactory excuse could be given. It was in the fall of the year, and at a time when the woods around Lewistown were full of nuts, wild fruit and grapes. So one day, during the noon spell, a dozen or fifteen of us took a stroll through the woods on the hunt of nuts and wild fruit. But it so happened that we ventured so far away that we did not get back until school had been taken up about half an hour. So, having broken one of the rules of the school, we all had to be punished. The boys were called up, one at a time, and each received four or five strokes across the back with a whip. There were three young ladies that were attending school who were in the company of the transgressors. Their ages ran from sixteen to eighteen, and the punishment meted out to them was that they were to go up into the judge's stand and climb up and stand upon the top of the judge's writing table. The young ladies were Miss Sally Laughton, daughter to John Laughton; Miss Nancy Johnson, daughter to William Johnson, who was one of the county commissioners, and Miss Susan Wentworth, daughter to Elijah Wentworth. They were amongst the most prominent families of the town. The young ladies were all quite tall, and as they stood in a row their heads extended up to the upper floor of the court house, and, as the floor had been laid with loose puncheons, the young ladies amused the scholars by raising up the ends of the puncheons on the top of their heads. This so amused one of the small boys that he laughed loud enough to be heard by the teacher, who called him up to punish him for his rudeness, when he excused himself by telling the teacher that he could not help laughing, for Sally Laughton kept tucking her head up in the loft. After they had stood about twenty minutes on their perch they were ordered to come down and to take their seats. They knew very well that it would not have done any good to have resisted the order of the schoolteacher, for if they had, they would have been whipped the same as the boys had been. Some of the smaller sized girls that were among the truants were let off by having to stand for a short time up on a bench. The teacher would have regarded himself as being recreant in his duty if he had let anyone escape punishment that had violated the rules of his school.

The first schoolhouse that was ever built in Lewistown or in Fulton county was built on a lot that stood immediately west of the public square. It was built of round logs 14x16 feet in size and covered with clapboards held down with heavy weight poles. The cracks in the walls were chinked and filled in with mud. The floors were laid down loose with hewed puncheons. The door was made of rough boards and hung on wooden hinges with wooden door-latch. There were two windows large enough for a sash containing six 8x10 glass, but as glass could not be obtained at that time, oiled paper was substituted for glass. A chimney was made of lath and made with a huge fireplace in one end of the house, large enough to contain a log two feet in diameter. The seats were made from a section of a log hewed on one side and wooden pins driven in auger holes for bench legs with no backs to rest the weary body against. The school was kept in this log schoolhouse some two years and until the log court house was built; the school was then transferred to the court house and a great day was manifested by teachers and scholars when the change was made. It was the custom in those times for the teacher to retain the scholars in school from eight to nine hours a day, and when I look back and think about how us poor urchins had to sit in those hard and rough benches during those long and weary hours with nothing to rest our tired backs against, I cannot help thinking that it was a most terrible cruel treatment.

CHAPTER XXIII.

LETTER FROM MR. JOHN W. PROCTOR.—MY REPLY THERETO.

Los Angeles, Cal., April 12.

Editor Democrat: Not long since I wrote to Mr. H. L. Ross of Oakland to thank him for the noble sketches he is writing for The Democrat, which have been so highly appreciated by all old residents of Illinois who have seen them. In my letter I mentioned the fact that I had attended his father's funeral (the late O. M. Ross); that Rev. Robt. Stewart of Canton came to my father's house in Lewistown on his way to attend Mr. Ross' funeral in Havana; that it was in mid-winter and very cold; that father hitched his horses to a box-sled, and Rev. Stewart, father, mother and myself, with sufficient buffalo robes, were soon ready for the long, cold ride, and that we crossed the Illinois river on the ice. I was then a boy of eight or nine. In his reply Mr. Ross has said many things of great interest to my relatives, and I think they will interest many pioneers. So I have his consent to print his letter. Few men have lived in Fulton county who have exerted a greater influence for good than H. L. Ross.

John W. Proctor.

MR. ROSS' LETTER.

Oakland, Cal., March 20.

Mr. John W. Proctor, Los Angeles, Cal.

My Dear Old Friend: I was very glad to get your good letter. It carried my mind back to the days of my youth. I very well remember that your father and mother attended the funeral of my father in 1837. Rev. Robt. Stewart of Canton came with them and preached the funeral sermon. The Illinois river had frozen over a few days before, and was not thought to be very safe. So your father walked across on the ice and got a spike pole out of the ferry boat and tried the ice, and then drove the horses and sleigh across the river, while he walked beside the sleigh, and Mr. Stewart and your mother walked a few rods behind the sleigh. I was attending college at Jacksonville at the time father died, but came home for the funeral. My brother Lewis was at Vandalia, and did not get home until five days after the funeral. Your father and mother were a very great help to us on that occasion.

Your father, as well as mine, was engaged in merchandizing. They went to St. Louis together one time to buy goods. As they were going from the hotel to take the steamboat, my father asked Mr. Proctor if he had insured his goods, and he said he had not; that he had hardly thought it worth while to do so. My father said he had insured his, and thought it the best policy. So Mr. Proctor turned about and went with my father to the insurance office and insured his goods. The boat started out that night, and had only gone sixteen miles up the river when she struck a snag and sunk to within six feet of the upper deck. The passengers all escaped. The next day you father and mine returned to St. Louis to draw their insurance money, which was promptly paid, and then the goods belonged to the insurance company. The officers of the insurance company told them they could have half of the goods they would save from the wreck. So they hired a couple of small keel-boats at St. Louis and a few men and went to the sunken boat where they worked about three weeks and recovered several thousand dollars' worth of goods. After an equal division of the goods and paying all expenses, they found that they had cleared above $1200 each from the enterprise, not a very bad investment after all.

While I lived in the village of Vermont in 1846 we organized a Presbyterian church with twelve members, and held our meetings in a log school house. We were anxious to buy a lot and build a better church; but we were all very poor, having no money to pay for the lot. About that time your father and mother came down on a visit to Mr. Heizer and family. Your father saw our condition, and very generously gave us $100 to buy the lot. Daniel Baughman, who lived ten miles north of Vermont, had a nice corner lot, which I bought of him for $65 for the church. When I left Vermont the church numbered 110 members, and their building still stands on the lot paid for by your honored father, William Proctor.

The first money I ever earned for myself was paid me by your father. My father had a large dog that got to killing sheep, and so he had him killed. So I concluded that I would skin the dog and sell the hide. I had watched my father and his men when they skinned cattle, and little as I was I thought I could skin the dog. So I got my sister Harriet to hold the legs while I did the skinning. So when we got him skinned I got a stick, and we spread the hide across it, I taking hold of one end and my sister the other, and started for the tanyard. We then lived where Major Newton Walker now lives, and it was about half a mile to your father's tanyard [the present site of Mr. Harben's vegetable garden in Lewistown—Ed.], so we trudged along, having to stop every few yards to rest, being such little tots. The dog skin was pretty heavy, as I had left considerable of the dog with the hide; but we finally got to the tanyard with it, and I asked your father how much he would give for it. He said as it was a large skin, and as we had worked so hard to bring it to him, he would give us a dollar, which was twenty-five cents above the price. So he paid me a dollar, and I divided it with my little sister, and I do not suppose that ever a little boy and girl went home feeling happier than we did.

When your father commenced the tanning business in Lewistown he took in two apprentices, Benjamin Scovil and John Nichols, who lived with him four years. Then John Nichols went to Galena, and from there to Los Angeles, Cal. I saw him there seventeen years ago. He was keeping a real estate office. He told me that he built the first frame house in Los Angeles; that he was its first mayor, and had held the office three terms. He at one time owned a very valuable ranch two or three miles from the city. He was an uncle to Judge H. L. Bryant's wife. He had a brother William, who lived five miles south of Canton on the Lewistown road. We often talked about the Lewistown people. We went to school together in the old log school house in Lewistown. He told me that he owed everything that was good about him to the moral and religious training he received from your father and mother. I thought if he was still living in Los Angeles you would like to look him up.

Yours truly,
H. L. Ross.

Abraham Lincoln.

CHAPTER I.

CONDITIONS UNDER WHICH I FIRST BECAME ACQUAINTED WITH ABRAHAM LINCOLN.

Editor of The Fulton Democrat: In earlier years I was intimately acquainted with Abraham Lincoln and Peter Cartwright, two of the old pioneers of Illinois, who lived in Sangamon County at the same time, and but a few miles apart, who took prominent part in molding the destiny and giving permanent prosperity to the state and nation. They have passed over the river and gone to their reward some thirty years ago, but for generations will their noble deeds and sacrifices be remembered and their sacred memory cherished deep down in the hearts of a grateful country and a generous people. There are probably but few men now living that knew Mr. Lincoln better than I did in the days of his obscurity, when he was trying to make an honest living by honest days' work. I believe that I knew about every occupation that he was engaged in from the time he came to New Salem until he was elected to Congress. Now I find, in reading historical sketches in the papers and magazines of the early life of Lincoln, also in some of his histories, a good many mistakes. Some of my old friends, and also my children and grandchildren, often ask me what I knew about Abraham Lincoln and Peter Cartwright, and I have decided to give the Fulton Democrat a few short historical sketches of what I knew about them in the old pioneer times. What I shall say shall be from my own personal knowledge and from what I know to be authentic and true; and I will endeavor to point out some of the errors and mistakes that I have alluded to.

Before I commence the narrative of the early life of Mr.

Lincoln it is likely some of the readers of the Democrat would like to know how I happened to become so well acquainted with such a distinguished person as Mr. Lincoln; and so I will have to make some explanation, and in doing so will have to state some circumstances connected with my own early life and occupations.

My father, Ossian M. Ross, settled in Havana in 1828. He kept the ferry across the Illinois river, built and kept the Havana Hotel, carried on a large farm, was a merchant and the postmaster, and in addition to those things he had the mail route from Springfield to Lewistown. The mail had to be carried twice a week on horseback, and I chose, rather than to work on the farm or in the store, to carry the mail. The postoffices between Lewistown and Springfield were Havana, New Salem, Athens and Sangamontown. Mr. Lincoln was postmaster at New Salem, where the mail had to be changed four times a week, and I put up at the log tavern where Mr. Lincoln boarded, and we partook of the cornbread, bacon and eggs, which were our common fare, at the same table. I would often assist Mr. Lincoln in his store and in sorting over the mail, and he would often send packages by me to his customers along the road; so my business required me to be with him a part of four days in every week. After he commenced the practice of law I got him to fix up my title papers to some land that came to me from my father's estate; and I have often met him when he was attending the circuit court in Mason county. The first court held in that county was at Havana; I was keeping the Havana Hotel at that time. There was no court house in the county, and the bar room of the hotel was used for a court room and some of my bed rooms for jury rooms. I remember Mr. Lincoln being engaged by Frank Low of Havana to prosecute Mr. Coon for slander. Mr. Lincoln got a judgment against Coon in favor of Low for some $500.

So the readers of The Democrat will see that I had a pretty good opportunity to learn something about Mr. Lincoln. I was also well acquainted with William H. Herndon, who was his law partner for twenty years, and who after his death wrote a history of his life. Mr. Herndon's father kept the Herndon Hotel in Springfield, and when I carried the mail I had to stop there two nights in each week. William and myself being near the same age (I being one year the older), we were a great deal together whenever I was in Springfield; we were also both in the Jacksonville college at the same time, in the same classes, and were roommates; and so I had a pretty good opportunity to know something about him. As I proceed with the narrative of what I know of the early life of Mr. Lincoln, I may also state what I know of the early life of Herndon, and point out some of the mistakes he has made in his "History of Lincoln."

CHAPTER II.

LINCOLN THE GROCERY CLERK.—HOW HE QUALIFIED HIMSELF FOR SURVEYOR.

The first time I ever saw or heard of Abraham Lincoln was in 1832. I had stopped over night at Jack Armstrong's, who lived on a farm five miles northwest of New Salem. I there saw a young man whom I had never met before, and asked him who he was, and he said his name was Abe Lincoln, and that he was working for his father. He was tall and slender, and was dressed in common homemade jeans, about the same kind of goods that the majority of the young men wore at that time—about the same as I wore myself. The next time I saw Lincoln, to become acquainted with him, was at the log tavern at New Salem, kept by James Rutledge. I was carrying the mail from Lewistown to Springfield, and put up with the Rutledge tavern where Mr. Lincoln was boarding. He was at that time a clerk in the store of Samuel Hill, a merchant of New Salem. Mr. Lincoln had been to New Orleans with a flat-boat load of produce, and Mr. Hill had sent by him 100 barrels of flour that was ground at the water mill at New Salem. Mr. Lincoln sold the flour at a good price, and was so prompt in paying the money, and gave such good satisfaction, that on his return Mr. Hill made him a clerk in his store. Mr. Hill had the largest stock of goods in New Salem, and also kept the postoffice. Mr. Lincoln, I observed, was always very attentive to business, and was kind and obliging to the customers of the store, always having pleasant things to say to them; and they had so much confidence in his honesty that they preferred to trade with him rather than with Mr. Hill or the other clerks. I noticed that this was particularly true of the women customers; they would often say that they liked to trade with Mr. Lincoln, for they believed that he was honest and would tell them the truth about the goods.

I went into the store one day to buy a pair of buckskin gloves and asked him if he had a pair that would fit me. He threw a pair on the counter. "There is a pair of dogskin gloves that I think will fit you, and you can have them for seventy-five cents." When he called them dogskin gloves I was surprised, as I had never heard of such a thing before. At that time no factory-made gloves had ever been brought into the country, and all the gloves and mittens that were worn were made by hand and by the women of the neighborhood, and were made from tanned deer skins, and the Indians usually did the tanning. A large buckskin, Indian dressed, could be bought at that time for from fifty to seventy-five cents. So I said to Mr. Lincoln, "How do you know they are dogskin gloves?" I believe that he thought my question was a little impudent, and it rasped him somewhat that I had the audacity to question his word. "Well, sir," said he, "I will tell you how I know they are dogskin gloves. Jack Clery's dog killed Tom Watkin's sheep, and Tom Watkin's boy killed the dog, and old John Mounts tanned the dogskin, and Sally Spears made the gloves, and that is how I know they are dogskin gloves." So I asked no more questions about the gloves, but paid the six bits and took them; and I can truly say that I have worn buckskin and dogskin gloves from time to time for sixty years since then, and have never found a pair that did me the service that those did I got of Mr. Lincoln.

I have understood that Mr. Lincoln got $20 a month for clerking in Mr. Hill's store, which was considered good wages at that time, although he had to pay $2 a week for his board.

While Mr. Lincoln was clerking in the store for $20 a month Mr. Hill gave him the privilege of going out to work in the time of harvest, where he could earn from $1 to $1.25 a day and his board; and when the harvest was over he would take him back in the store again.

In the fall of 1835 my brother Lewis was a student in the Jacksonville college. I had to take him back to college after the vacation, and there met many of the boys who had returned after their two months' rest. Among these was Richard Yates, afterwards the great "war governor" of Illinois. Most of these boys had been at work during the vacation—most of them on their father's farm, while some of them had taught school, and others clerked in the stores. Among them was a young man named William Green, who said he had been at home helping his father with the harvest. While there a young man named Abe Lincoln had come out from New Salem to help with the harvest. He said Lincoln could pitch more hay than any man his father had. When Lincoln found out that young Green had been to college he asked him if he had brought his books home with him. He said he had never had the advantage of an education, and said he would like to study grammar and arithmetic, and asked if Green would assist him, and he told him that he would. Mr. Lincoln said that the county surveyor at Springfield, Mr. Calhoun, had been talking of appointing him deputy surveyor if he would qualify himself for the place. He was very anxious to get the position, as there was a good deal of surveying to be done around New Salem. So Lincoln would get up early in the morning and feed the horses, and then with the help of Green would go at the grammar and arithmetic until breakfast was ready. At night they would again resume their studies. After Lincoln returned to the store in New Salem, Green would take his books when he went to town, and they would study together under the shade of the trees. Green said he never saw another person who could learn as fast as Lincoln did. It is a fact that Mr. Lincoln did qualify himself and was appointed deputy surveyor; and he was one of the best surveyors they ever had in that part of the country.

This William Green in 1875 moved to Warren county, Illinois, some five miles from Avon, and for several years was president of the Avon Agricultural Society. Not long after I visited him, and he told me that he had gone to Washington to see Lincoln while he was president. He said Lincoln was glad to see him, throwing his arms about his neck and showing him many marks of kindness while he remained in the city. Before he came away Mr. Lincoln introduced him to some of his cabinet officers, telling them that he was the young man who taught him grammar and arithmetic in his father's barn.

I have not heard from Mr. Green in eighteen years; but if he is still living he can tell more of the early life of Abraham Lincoln than can be found in any of the papers, magazines or histories.

CHAPTER III.

SOME ERRORS IN HERNDON'S "LIFE OF LINCOLN."— ANNE RUTLEDGE, LINCOLN'S FIRST SWEETHEART, AND HER UNTIMELY DEATH.

The town of New Salem, where I became acquainted with Lincoln, was laid out in 1829 by John Cameron and George Rutledge on a high piece of ground overlooking the Sangamon river, and was surrounded by fine farming country. It was twenty miles northwest of Springfield; had some fifty houses, about one-third frame and the balance log; there were four stores, postoffice, log tavern, a blacksmith and wagon maker's shop, a carding machine, and a water mill on the Sangamon river.

A few months after Mr. Lincoln took the postoffice, finding that the revenue would not support him, he took a young man named William Berry in partnership with him and opened a general country store. The stock consisted chiefly of groceries, but they also had many notions, hats, mittens, etc. The entire stock could not have been worth over $1200. The charge has been made that Mr. Lincoln took out a license and kept a saloon in the store. Indeed, Judge Douglas in his debate with Lincoln occasionally charged Lincoln that he had been engaged in the saloon business. Lincoln's reply was that he had never kept a saloon, and that he had never sold a glass of liquor over a counter; but that if he ever had run a saloon, and Douglas had lived in that neighborhood, he would undoubtedly have been his best customer.

I am sure that no liquor was sold by the drink in their store while Mr. Lincoln had an interest in it. I had occasion to be in the store very often while I was carrying the mail, and had a much better opportunity to know what was going on there than did William H. Herndon, who wrote a story of Lincoln's life, but who lived twenty miles away from New Salem. I think that it is likely they did sell whisky by the quart and gallon, as was done in every pioneer store. Indeed, whisky was as common an article of barter as was coffee, sugar or tea. The pioneers were subject to much sickness, caused by malarial conditions—fever and ague, typhoid fever, etc. A favorite remedy was bitters made from barks and roots and whisky. At that time the country was full of poisonous snakes, and it was a common thing for people to be bitten. The one remedy in those days was to fill up the patient with whisky. The whisky used at that time was the pure juice of the corn or rye, and could be bought at fifty cents a gallon. We had none of that vile, poisonous stuff that is now made from drugs and kept for sale in the saloons.

In all my acquaintance with Mr. Lincoln I never knew him to take a drink of liquor of any kind, nor use tobacco in any form, or ever to use profane language. His earliest biographer, W. H. Herndon, claimed that Lincoln did drink whisky and swear. It is claimed that the swearing was done in New Orleans, where he had gone with a flat boat full of produce, and where he attended an auction sale of negroes and saw a young woman two-thirds white being sold. It was then that Mr. Lincoln expressed his indignation by an oath. The time when it was claimed that he drank liquor was when he was said to have lifted a barrel of whisky to his lips and drank out of the bung hole. I am inclined to believe that my old college chum and roommate, W. H. Herndon, drew largely on his imagination when he told these stories.

At this time Mr. Lincoln boarded at the Rutledge tavern, at which I also put up, as often as I went to New Salem. It was a hewed log house, two stories high, with four rooms above and four below. It had two chimneys with large fireplaces, and not a stove in the house. The proprietor was James Rutledge, a man of more than ordinary ability, and, with his wife, remarkably kind and hospitable. They had a large family of eight or nine children, and among them was their daughter Anne, celebrated in song and story as Lincoln's sweetheart. She was two or three years younger than Lincoln, of about medium size, weighing some 125 pounds. She was very handsome and attractive, as well as industrious and sweet-spirited. I seldom saw her when she was not engaged in some occupation—knitting, sewing, waiting on table, etc. I think she did the sewing for the entire family. Lincoln was boarding at the tavern and fell deeply in love with Anne, and she was no less in love with him. They were engaged to be married, but they had been putting off the wedding for a while, as he wanted to accumulate a little more property and she wanted to go longer to school.

Before the time came when they were to be married, Miss Anne was taken down with typhoid fever and lay desperately ill four weeks. Lincoln was an anxious and constant watcher at her bedside. The sickness ended in her death; and young Lincoln was heartbroken and prostrated. The histories have not exaggerated his pitiful grief. For many days he was not able to attend to business. I believe his very soul was wrapped up in that lovely girl. It was his first love—the holiest thing in life—the love that cannot die. The deepest gloom and melancholy settled over his mind. He would often say to his friends: "My heart is buried in the grave with that dear girl." He would often go and sit by her grave and read a little pocket Testament he carried with him. What did he read? I know not; but I'll warrant you that it was "Let not your hearts be troubled," or John's vision on Patmos with Anne among the white-robed throng in the land where sickness and death are unknown. One stormy winter's night he was at a friend's house, and as the sleet and rain came down on the roof he sat with bowed head and the tears trickled down his face. His friends begged him to control his sorrow. "I cannot," he moaned, "while storm and darkness are on her grave." His friends did everything that kindness could suggest, but in vain, to soothe his sorrow.

Anne Rutledge was of gentle blood, she would have made him a noble wife in his humbler earlier years and in the imperial later life. Miss Anne's brother David took a course in Jacksonville College, and then went to Lewistown and studied law in the office of Lewis W. Ross and John P. Boice. He married Miss Elizabeth Simms, daughter of Colonel Reuben Simms, and he afterwards moved to Petersburg and opened a law office. He was a bright and promising man, and no doubt would have made his mark in state and nation but for his untimely death. He was buried by the side of his sister Anne in the New Salem cemetery. *Or Concord Cem,*

His widow married C. W. Andrus, one of the prominent merchants of Havana. Major Newton Walker, L. W. Ross and James W. Simms all married sisters to Mrs. David Rutledge.

The Rutledge family stood high in the Sangamon country. Anne's father was a South Carolinian of high birth. One of his family signed the Declaration of Independence; another was chief justice of the supreme court under Washington's appointment, and a third was a conspicuous leader in Congress. So Lincoln's boyhood love was of high and gentle birth.

CHAPTER IV.

LINCOLN'S SECOND SWEETHEART, MARY OWENS.—HIS LETTER IN REGARD TO THE BREAKING OF THE ENGAGEMENT.—FIRST CIRCUS OF PIONEER DAYS.

One year after the sad death of Anne Rutledge, Mr. Lincoln again fell in love. Miss Mary Owens was his second sweetheart. She came from Kentucky on a visit to a married sister who lived near New Salem. In many respects she was very different from Anne Rutledge. She was older and larger; she was finely educated, and had been brought up in the most refined society, and she dressed much finer than any of the ladies who lived about New Salem. Her fashionable silk dresses, kid shoes and leghorn hat were in striking contrast with the calico dress, calfskin shoes and straw bonnet that Anne had worn.

Miss Owens was in the habit of making frequent visits to the postoffice for letters from her Kentucky home, and that was where Lincoln first became acquainted with her. It was not very long until he began to be a frequent visitor at her sister's home, and these visits continued until her return to Kentucky. It became the gossip of the neighborhood that they were to be married. When the gossip was repeated to Lincoln by a friend he replied: "If ever that girl comes back to New Salem I am going to marry her in about three years." Miss Mary did, in due time, return, but Mr. Lincoln did not marry her, and I presume the reader will want to know the secret of it all. They did not agree, and she would not consent to the marriage. On this point Miss Mary is reported to have said that there were many things about Mr. Lincoln that she liked, and many other things she did not like, and the things she did not like overbalanced the things she did like. "I could not help admiring Mr. Lincoln," she said, "for his honesty, truthfulness and sincerity and goodness of heart; but I think he was a little too presumptuous when he told his friend that if I ever came back to New Salem he was going to marry me. That is a bargain that it takes two to make; and then his training and bringing up had been so different from my own and his awkward and uncouth behavior was most disagreeable. He was lacking in those little links which make up the chain of woman's happiness. At least that was my judgment. He was not the ideal husband that I had pictured to myself that I could love, and so, when he asked me to become his wife, I told him no."

Now I will give Mr. Lincoln's side of the story. He had a dear lady friend whom he confided in and advised with in many of his private affairs. She had learned that he was engaged to Miss Mary and that the engagement had been broken off, and she wanted to know the cause. So he wrote her a letter, and it is presumable that he did not expect the letter to go out of her possession, unless it went into the fire; but as time went on it did get out of her possession and the following is a copy of it:

"SPRINGFIELD, April 1st, 1838.

"*Dear Madam:*—It was in the autumn of 1836 that a married lady of my acquaintance, and who was a great friend of mine, being about to pay a visit to her father and other relatives residing in Kentucky, proposed to me that on her return she would bring a sister of hers with her on condition that I would engage to become her brother-in-law. With all convenient dispatch I, of course, accepted the proposal, for you know that I would not have done otherwise had I really been averse to it; but, privately between you and me, I was most confoundedly well pleased with the project. I had seen the said sister some three years before; thought her intelligent and agreeable, and saw no good objection to plodding life through hand in hand with her. Time passed on. The lady took her journey and in due time returned, her sister in company, sure enough. This astonished me a little, for it appeared to me that her coming so readily showed that she was a trifle too willing. But on reflection it occurred to me that she might have been prevailed on by her married sister to come without anything concerning me ever having been mentioned to her; and so I concluded that if no other objection presented itself I would consent to waive this. All this occurred to me on hearing of her arrival in the neighborhood, for, be it remembered, I had not yet seen her except about three years previous, as above mentioned. In a few days we had an interview, and, although I had seen her before, she did not look as my imagination had pictured her. I knew she was over size, but she now appeared a fair match for Falstaff. I know she was called an old maid, and I felt no doubt of the truth of at least half of the appellation. But now, when I beheld her I could not for my life avoid thinking of my mother; and this not from her withered features, for her skin was too full of fat to permit of it contracting into wrinkles; but from her want of teeth and weather-beaten appearance in general, and from a kind of notion that ran in my head that nothing could have commenced at the size of infancy and reached her present bulk in less than thirty-five or forty years. In short, I was not at all pleased with her; but what could I do? I had told her sister I would take her for better or for worse; and made it a point of honor and conscience in all things to stick to my word, especially if others had been induced to act on it, which in this case I had no doubt they had. I was now fully convinced that no other man on earth would have her, and hence the conclusion that they were bent on holding me to my bargain. Well, thought I, I have said it, and be the consequences what they may be it shall not be my fault if I fail to do it. At once I determined to consider her my wife, and, this done, all my powers of discovery were put to work in search of perfections in her which might be fairly set off against her defects. I tried to imagine her handsome, which but for her unfortunate corpulency was actually true; exclusive of this no woman that I had ever seen had a fairer face. I also tried to convince myself that the mind was much more to be valued than the person; and in this she was not inferior, as I could discover, to any with whom I had been acquainted. Shortly after this, without coming to any positive understanding with her, I set out for Vandalia to take my seat in the legislature to which I had been elected. During my stay there I had letters from her which did not change my opinion of her intellect or intention; but, on the contrary, confirmed it in both. All this while, although I was fixed firm as the surge-repelling rock in my resolution, I found that I was continually repenting the rashness that had led me to make it. After my return home I saw nothing to change my opinion of her in any particulars. She was the same, and so was I. I now spent my time in planning how I might get along in life after my contemplated change of circumstances should have taken place, and how I might procrastinate the evil day for a time, which I really dreaded, as much, perhaps more, than an Irishman does the halter. After all my suffering upon this deeply interesting subject, here I am wholly, unexpectedly and completely out of the scrape. And now I want to know if you can guess how I got out of it—out clear in every sense of the term—no violation of word, honor or conscience? I do not believe you can guess, and so I might as well tell you at once. As the lawyer says, it was done in the manner following, to wit: After I had delayed the matter as long as I thought I could in honor do, I concluded I might as well bring it to a consummation without further delay, and so I mustered my resolution and made the proposal to her direct; but, shocking to relate, she answered No. At first I supposed she did so through an affectation of modesty, which I thought but ill-becoming her under the peculiar circumstances of her case. But on my renewal of the charge I found that she repelled it with greater firmness than before. I tried it again and again, but with the same success, or rather, with the same want of success. I finally was forced to give it up, at which very unexpectedly I found myself mortified almost beyond endurance. I was mortified, it seems to me, in a hundred different ways. My vanity was deeply wounded by the reflection that I had been too stupid to discover her intentions, and at the same time never doubting that I understood them perfectly; and, also, that she whom I had taught myself to believe of all women would have been the last to reject me with all my greatness. And, to cap the whole, I then for the first time began to suspect that I was really a little bit in love with her. But let it all go. I'll try and outlive it. Others have been made fools of by the girls, but this can never with truth be said of me. I most emphatically in this instance made a fool of myself. I have now come to the conclusion never again to think of marrying, and for this reason: I can never be satisfied with anyone who would be blockheaded enough to have me.

"Your sincere friend,
"A. LINCOLN."

The above mentioned Miss Mary Owens was afterwards married to a highly respectable gentleman and became the mother of five children. She died July 4, 1877. Speaking of Mr. Lincoln a short time before her death she said of him: "He was a man with a heart full of kindness and a head full of sense."

In the summer of 1833 the first circus and menagerie ever known in the West was billed to be in Springfield. I was then carrying the mail from Springfield to Lewistown, and Mr. Lincoln was keeping the postoffice at New Salem. The putting up of the circus bills created intense excitement in all the Springfield country. Thousands of the pioneers, as well as myself, had never seen such a show. Although I lived forty miles away I was determined, if possible, to go to Springfield and see the wonderful parade (advertised to take place on the streets at 12 o'clock), and also to see the show. I started at 12 o'clock the preceding night on horseback, and got to New Salem just at sunup the next morning. I went to the Rutledge tavern to get my breakfast and have my horse fed, and was told by Mr. Rutledge that Mr. Lincoln had gone to the country the day before to do some surveying, and he had not returned; and that Bill Berry, his partner, had been to a dance the night before, and that it did not break up until near daylight, and that Bill had filled up pretty well on eggnogg, and he feared I would have some trouble in waking him up to change the mail so I could go on with my journey. After breakfast I found Bill in a profound slumber in a little room adjoining the postoffice. For half an hour I pounded at the door, and hallooed and yelled, but all in vain. It would have taken Gabriel's trump to have waked him up. So I had to throw my mail-bags across my horse and pursue my journey—or I would miss that wonderful parade.

At Sangamontown (seven miles beyond New Salem) I told the postmaster about my trouble at New Salem and asked him to keep the New Salem mail until my return next day, when I would carry it back. He did so, and I hurried on, and got to Springfield in time to see the parade and show. There was a mighty host of people in town who had come from far and near. Some had come as far as twenty miles in ox teams, fetching their entire families. There probably has never been so much excitement in Springfield from the time it was laid out as a town until now, except upon two other events. The first was when Lincoln the year before had piloted the little steamboat, the Talisman, up the Sangamon river and landed her at the bank near Springfield. The people believed that the Sangamon river would always be navigable for steamboats, and were wild with excitement and enthusiasm over the glorious outlook for the town's assured prosperity. The other great excitement was when the State capital was moved from Vandalia to Springfield. I may more fully allude to these other two events in a future sketch.

There were two things connected with the show that astonished the people most wonderfully. One was the monster anaconda, a serpent eighteen feet long, and the other was the young lady that stood upon her feet on the back of a horse and rode at full speed around the ring. If there was anything that would bring fear and terror to the early settlers it was the sight of a big snake. They had seen so many cases where people had been bitten by snakes, and the terrible sufferings they had endured, that they had a good reason to abhor and dread a snake. So when the showman took the monster from the iron cage, and it crawled upon his shoulder, with its hideous head extended far above him, and with its forked tongue darting out six inches, and its baneful eyes that looked like two balls of fire, the big audience was transfixed with terror. But when the showman commenced to carry the hideous thing about the ring close to the people, the women commenced screaming and the children crying in chorus, and the men commenced to yell for the snake to be shut up in the cage. And so the showman had to stop the horrid performance and put the anaconda back into the iron cage, or there would have been a general stampede from the big tent. But the people cautiously thereafter approached the cage to gaze upon the dreadful snake.

The people were entranced with the spangled young woman that rode at full speed about the ring, standing upon the horse's back. It was a common sight to see women and girls driving horses while they held the plow, or see them on horseback on a grist of corn going many miles to the water mills. The pioneer girls and women, as a rule, were expert horse-women on a side-saddle, or even bare-back. But when it came to a pretty girl standing on a horse going at full speed, it took their breath and made their hearts stand still. No mortal of them could ever have believed that a girl could do a thing like that until they saw it. There had been no rain in the Springfield country for several weeks, and the black dust lay deep in all the roads and streets. The big crowds kept it stirred up, and the women and children in their holiday clothes were a sight to behold.

I learned that Lincoln had got back to New Salem a few hours after I passed through, and was a little displeased because I had not left the mail, not knowing the cause. With every man, woman and child that could pay his way in, Mr. Lincoln went to the show. After the show was over I met Lincoln on the street, and as we met I noticed a little scowl on his face. He said to me: "How did it happen that you came through New Salem and did not have the mail changed? You might get me into trouble about this. Suppose the postmaster at Springfield should report the fact to the department at Washington that the mail was not opened at New Salem, but was brought on to Springfield, what would happen to me?"

Then I told him the whole story, how I had got up at 12 o'clock at night so that I could get to Springfield to see the show come into town, and that I had never seen a show, and how anxious I was to see it, and how hard I had tried to get Bill Berry up to open the mail, and that I had not brought the mail to Springfield but had left it at Sangamontown and would carry it back to New Salem in the morning. Then Mr. Lincoln in a kind voice said: "O, well, in that case it is all right. Bill Berry ought to have got up and opened the mail for you." Then he said: "I am going home this evening, and I will stop and get the mail and carry it home with me," which I found next day that he had done.

When I met Lincoln I noticed that he had bought a new suit of clothes and a new hat, and while he stood talking with me I had a good opportunity to scrutinize his whole wardrobe, and I believe I can remember every article of his clothing as well as if I had only seen it yesterday. The coat and pants were of brown linen and the vest of white marseilles with dots of flowers in it. The shirt was open front with small pleats buttoned up with small ivory buttons. The collar was wide and folded over the collar of his coat. He had for a necktie a black silk handkerchief with a narrow fringe to it, and it was tied in a double bow knot. He wore a pair of low shoes with a narrow ribbon fastened on each side of the shoes, and they were tied in a double bow knot over the instep. He wore a buckeye hat, made of splints from the buckeye tree, and much after the fashion of straw hats. These buckeye hats were much worn in those times, and cost twice as much as the straw hats, or $1.25 to $1.50 each. So the reader may see how Mr. Lincoln must have looked when he was dressed up for the circus.

When I got back to New Salem next morning I found that Lincoln had given the people their mail, and that Bill Berry had got sober and was very sorry for his misconduct, and that Lincoln had washed off the Springfield black dust and was amiable and happy as ever.

CHAPTER V.

LINCOLN'S TRIP ON A FLATBOAT TO NEW ORLEANS.—HIS VISIT TO A SLAVE MARKET, AND HIS AVOWED HATRED AND INTENTION REGARDING THE INSTITUTION OF SLAVERY.

In getting up these little sketches of the life of Mr. Lincoln it is not my intention to go into a general history of his life, for after he was elected to the Legislature in 1834 his grand and noble life was an open book and is known and read by all men, but to speak of those little things that led him up step by step to that honorable and noble life. It may be an encouragement for many young men to follow his example.

The first thing he undertook after coming to Illinois, worth mentioning, and that started him on his way to the White House, was his trip down the Sangamon river on a flat boat loaded down with produce. He was twenty-one years old, dressed in buckskin pants, butternut colored jeans coat, checked shirt and straw hat. If a casual observer had been told that the young man was starting for the White House at Washington he would probably have said such a thing was impossible. But nevertheless such were the facts of the case, for inside of that checked shirt and jeans coat was an honest, generous and noble heart; inside of that straw hat was a head filled with good, solid horse sense, and the good Lord had blessed him with an indomitable will, a sound body, a good pair of eyes and a good memory. He commenced using his eyes and memory as soon as the boat started down the stream. He spied out snags, sandbars, overhanging trees and other obstructions to navigation and remembered them, which secured him the position of pilot on a steamboat that ran up the Sangamon river the next year. His boat floated down the Sangamon, Illinois and Mississippi rivers to New Orleans, where he sold boat and produce for a good price. He remained there long enough to visit the slave market and to see husbands and wives, parents and children torn from each other's arms to be separated perhaps forever. These things he also remembered, and when turning away he said to his companion, "If ever I get a chance I will strike that thing, and I will strike it hard"—meaning the institution of slavery. As time rolled on his opportunity to strike came and the slaves were freed!

He went to the steamboat landing to take passage for St. Louis, but instead of paying $40 for a passage and spending his time drinking, smoking and playing cards as the other young men did, he went to the captain and asked him if he wanted another hand on the boat. The captain told him to come around the next morning and he could have work, so he got his passage free and made a nice little sum of money besides. When he got to St. Louis he found the Illinois river steamboat had just left and that there would not be another one going for several days. He left his baggage with his partner and went across the country to Coles county to visit his parents, but did not stay long, as he was anxious to return to New Salem and turn over the money to the man who had shipped the produce. That transaction showed the people that he was capable and honest and he immediately received employment as a clerk and was afterwards appointed postmaster and county surveyor. This was another step towards the White House.

The next spring he was looking over a newspaper and saw that a steamboat was to come up the Illinois river with the intention of running up the Sangamon as far as Springfield. Learning what time she would reach Beardstown Mr. Lincoln set out afoot for that place, and when the steamboat Talisman landed and threw out her gang plank, he was the first person to step on board. He offered his services to pilot the boat up the Sangamon river, telling the captain that he had navigated that stream in a flat boat and knew where all the obstructions were, so he was secured to pilot the boat to Springfield and back for $50. The running of a steamboat on the Sangamon river caused a wonderful excitement in Springfield, and, in fact, in all the country round about, for at that time no railroads had been built and the merchants and farmers had to haul their goods and produce to and from St. Louis, a distance of ninety-five miles. It took from ten days to two weeks to make a trip, but now they were to have a market right at home.

When the legislature had passed a law a few years before declaring the Sangamon a navigable stream, little was thought of it. Now Lincoln had taken a flatboat load of produce down the river and had brought a steamboat up, which demonstrated the fact to a certainty that Sangamon river was a navigable stream. Great crowds of people came from all parts of the country to see her, as few had ever seen a steamboat. She laid at the wharf near Springfield a week and during that time Lincoln was the hero of the occasion. He took advantage of this by getting acquainted with the people, making several speeches and shaking hands with every one. He got acquainted with more people during that one week than he could have met in three months in traveling around the country. It was on this occasion that Mr. Lincoln's friends brought him out for the legislature. There was another circumstance connected with the running of the steamboat up the Sangamon that benefited Mr. Lincoln. It induced almost every man who had land above high water to have it laid out in town lots, and Mr. Lincoln got several fat jobs of surveying.

Mr. Lincoln had become very popular among the people because he had been so fair and honorable in all his dealings, and he would no doubt have been elected to the legislature had not the Democrats put up grand old Peter Cartwright, the Methodist circuit rider and camp-meeting orator. Cartwright had the advantage because he had preached in every church and school house and at every camp-meeting in the county and had lived in the county six years longer than Lincoln. He also had the advantage in age, being forty-seven years old, while Lincoln was but twenty-three. Cartwright had served a term in the legislature and was one of the best members in that body, therefore the people sent him back by a small majority over Lincoln. That was the only time Lincoln was ever beaten for office, and the only time Cartwright was ever beaten for office was by Lincoln in 1846, when they were running for

Congress. It was unfortunate for the people that both of these noble men could not have been elected. Peter Cartwright was a simon pure Andrew Jackson Democrat and Abraham Lincoln was a Henry Clay Whig.

CHAPTER VI.

THE FIRST STEP TO THE WHITE HOUSE.—THE "SHIRTSLEEVE COURT IN THE CORN FIELD."—MR. LINCOLN'S REFUSAL OF A WELL-EARNED FEE.

In my last week's sketch of Lincoln I wanted to emphasize the fact that his trip to New Orleans in a flatboat, when he first saw in that city the horrors of slavery, was the first round in the ladder that led him to the president's chair. If he had not gone to New Orleans he would never have seen husbands and wives and parents and little children separated forever at the auction block, and it is not likely that his great heart would ever have been fired as it was with a deathless hatred of "the infamy of infamies."

Then if he had not gone with a flatboat down the Sangamon en route to New Orleans, he would never have piloted that steamboat up the Sangamon to Springfield. It was this incident that put him on the track for the legislature. That step logically led him on to Congress, then to fight with Douglas for a seat in the senate, then to the triumphant march to the presidency. It was all step by step on the ladder of fame from the flatboat to the president's chair.

I had a quarter section of land, two miles south of Macomb, that came to me from my father's estate. It was a fine quarter, but there was a little defect in the title, which could be remedied by the evidence of a man named Hagerty, who lived six miles west of Springfield and who knew the facts I wished to prove. I had noticed in the papers that court was in session at Springfield, and as court convened but twice a year I immediately started for that place, which was sixty miles from my home. I found my witness and took him with me. On arriving at Springfield we went directly to Mr. Lincoln's office, which was over a store on the west side of the square. I think the office was about fourteen feet square and contained two tables, two book cases and four or five chairs, while the floor was perfectly bare. I told Mr. Lincoln my business and showed him my title papers, which he looked over and then remarked to me, " I am sorry to have to tell you that you are a little too late, for this court adjourned this morning and does not convene again for six months, and Judge Thomas has gone home. He lives on his farm a mile east of the public square, but," said he, " we will go and see him and see if anything can be done for you." I told him I would get a carriage and we would drive out, but he said, " No; I can walk if you can." I said I would just as soon walk as ride, and before we started he pulled off his coat and laid it on a chair, taking from the pocket a large bandana silk handkerchief to wipe the perspiration from his face, as it was a very warm day in August. He struck off across the public square in his shirt sleeves with the red handkerchief in one hand and my bundle of papers in the other while my witness and I followed.

We soon came to Judge Thomas' residence, which was a one-story frame house. Mr. Lincoln knocked at the door— at that time there were no door bells—and the judge's wife came to the door. Mr. Lincoln asked if the judge was at home and she replied that he had gone to the north part of the farm, where they had a tenant house, to help his men put up a corn crib. She said if we went the main road it would be about a half-mile, but we could cut across the corn field and it would not be more than a quarter of a mile. Mr. Lincoln said if she would show us the path we would take the short cut, so she came out of the house and showed us where a path struck off across the field from their barn. We followed this path, Mr. Lincoln.in the lead, and myself and witness following in Indian file, and soon came to where the judge and his men were raising a log house about 12x20 feet in size, which was to serve as a corn crib and hog house. Mr. Lincoln told Judge Thomas how I had come from Fulton county and brought my witness to town just after court had adjourned, and said he thought he would come out and see if anything could be done. The judge looked over the title papers and said he guessed they could fix it up, so he swore my witness, with whom he was acquainted, and procuring a pen and ink from his tenant fixed the papers.

The judge and all the balance of us were in our shirt sleeves, and Mr. Lincoln remarked to the judge that it was a kind of a shirt-sleeve court. "Yes," replied the judge, "a shirt-sleeve court in a corn field." After the business had been transacted Mr. Lincoln asked Judge Thomas if he did not want some help in rolling up the logs, and the judge replied that there were two logs that were pretty heavy and he would like to have us help roll them up. So before we left we helped roll these logs logs up, Mr. Lincoln steering one end and the judge the other. I offered to pay the judge for taking the deposition of my witness, but he said he guessed I had helped with the raising enough to pay for that and would take nothing for his work. When we got back to Lincoln's office in town I think we had walked at least three miles. Mr. Lincoln put my papers in a large envelope with the name "Stuart & Lincoln" printed at the top. "Now," said he, "when you go home put those papers on record and you will have a good title to your land."

I then took out my pocket book to pay him and supposed he would charge me about $10, as I knew he was always moderate in his charges. "Now, Mr. Lincoln," said I, "how much shall I pay you for this work and the long walk through the hot sun and dust?" He paused for a moment and took the big silk handkerchief and wiped the perspiration off that was running down his face, and said: "I guess I will not charge you anything for that. I will let it go on the old score." When he said that it broke me all up and I could not keep the tears from running down my face, for I could recall many instances where he had been so good and kind to me when I was carrying the mail; then for him to say he would charge me nothing for this work was more kindness than I could stand. I suppose that what he meant by the old score was that I had occasionally helped him in his store and postoffice and my father had assisted him some when he got the postoffice.

Now, there is something a little remarkable in the history of those two men who worked together rolling up those two logs. It showed that the prominent men of that time were not too proud to engage in common labor. Judge Jesse B. Thomas, who was engaged at one end of the log, had served as representative in the Territorial Legislature of Illinois, had been twice elected to the United States Senate, once as a supreme judge, and was a member of the constitutional convention that framed the first constitution of Illinois, and had done more and had exerted a greater influence toward making the State of Illinois a slave state than any other man. While the man at the other end of the log was Abraham Lincoln, who afterwards served in the Legislature, in Congress, and as President of the United States, and who did more to banish slavery from the United States than any other man.

CHAPTER VII.

HOW LINCOLN FIRST EARNED THE SOBRIQUET OF "HONEST ABE."—HIS SPEECH WINS THE DEBATE.—CIRCUMSTANCES OF HIS SPEECH IN 1858 WHEN RUNNING FOR SENATOR.

When Mr. Lincoln first commenced the practice of law there was nothing that brought him so prominently before the people as a lawyer as his punctuality in collecting debts for his clients and paying over the money.

At that time about two-thirds of all the business was done on credit. The Illinois merchants would buy their goods from the Eastern and St. Louis wholesale merchants on twelve months' credit and sell them to the farmers and mechanics on the same time. The consequence was that the merchant's note would not be paid and it would be sent to some lawyer for collection, and then there would be as much trouble to get the money from the lawyers as it was from the customer. But Mr. Lincoln, whenever he collected any money, immediately forwarded it to the creditor, and in that way built up a practice that extended over several counties and earned for him the name of "Honest Abe" Lincoln.

I remember meeting Mr. Lincoln, in the spring of 1839, between Canton and Lewistown. I overtook him about two miles north of Lewistown, and as we rode along he told me he had been attending court in Knox and Warren counties and was on his way back to Springfield. As it was late in the afternoon and the roads were muddy, Mr. Lincoln said he would stay in Lewistown over night, and inquired about the taverns. I directed him to Truman Phelps' tavern, as it was the best place, and he stayed there over night. I remember he had a large pair of portmanteaus on his saddle which appeared to be pretty well filled. I suppose he had his law books and some clothing in them, for at that time lawyers who traveled around the circuit carried their law books with them. He was dressed in a suit of Kentucky jeans, over which was a heavy overcoat having four capes and a standing collar and fastening with a hook and clasp. He also wore a pair of green baize leggings, wrapped two or three times around the leg and tied just below the knee and pinned at the top and bottom.

The night Mr. Lincoln stayed in Lewistown happened to be the evening for the regular meeting of the Lewistown lyceum, and he attended. The meetings of the lyceum were largely attended by both the ladies and gentlemen of the town and were held in the old Methodist church, two blocks west of the court house. The subject for discussion that evening was "Which has done the most for the establishment and maintenance of our republican form of government and free institutions, the sword or pen?" and Mr. Lincoln was invited to take part in the debate, which he did. The men speaking on the side of the sword were Lewis W. Ross, Richard Johnson and Joseph Sharp, all lawyers, and those speaking for the pen were J. P. Boice and Abraham Lincoln, both lawyers, and William Kelly, a merchant of Lewistown. The speakers for the sword commenced with George Washington and ran down to General Jackson and General Cass and other officers who had gained great victories by the sword. When Lincoln commenced his speech he eulogized the other side for the effort they had made but said they had omitted the name of one of the valiant generals who lived in their own country. "For instance," said he, "there is General Stillman, who led the volunteers in the Black Hawk war." When he mentioned the name of General Stillman a smile came over the face of every one present, for we all remembered the general's defeat, and how Black Hawk, with his little band of Indians, chased him, with his larger force, fifteen miles and drove them into Fort Dixon. After Mr. Lincoln had joked them a little about their generals he entered into the subject in earnest and quoted from the writings of Patrick Henry, Benjamin Franklin and many other great men, which showed that he was well posted in the writings and history of our country. He made a royal good speech and the judges awarded to his side the victory, much to the gratification of Messrs. Boice and Kelly.

Mr. Lincoln was dressed in a suit of jeans with heavy boots and looked like a farmer, and the people were very much surprised when they heard his speech. A number of ladies attended that evening and I had walked over to the meeting with Miss Isabella Johnson, who remarked that she thought the rough, farming looking man had made the best speech. Attorney Johnson, who was one of Lincoln's opponents in that debate, and who was familiarly known as "Dick" Johnson, came to California in 1850 and was elected attorney general of the state and held several other important offices. He came to see me after I came to California and in talking over old times asked me if I remembered the time he and Lincoln measured the sword against the pen in the old Methodist church in Lewistown. He said he little thought that the man who defeated him in that debate would some day become President of the United States.

Mr. Lincoln was well posted in all that took place in the Black Hawk war, for he enlisted three times. The first time the volunteers were called out by Governor Reynolds it was for three months and Mr. Lincoln was elected Captain of his company. After the company was discharged it re-enlisted and served its time out and was again discharged, when Mr. Lincoln again re-enlisted and served until the close of the war.

I remember the circumstances connected with Mr. Lincoln's speech in Lewistown in August 1858, when he was running for United States Senator against Stephen A. Douglas. I was then living at Vermont, twenty miles from Lewistown, and drove to the latter town with my wife. She had often heard me speak of Mr. Lincoln and of his kindness to me when I was a lad carrying the mail, and she wanted to see him and hear him speak. I might say right here that we have been married for almost fifty-seven years, and that is the only political meeting she has ever had a disposition to attend. We stopped at my brother Lewis' house and found Mr. Lincoln sitting on the west porch. He and my brother Lewis had served together in the legislature and he had called at my brother's home to see him. I shook hands with him and told him that my wife and I had driven twenty miles that morning to hear him speak.

Mr. Lincoln delivered his address in front of the old court house on a platform erected between two pillars. There were seats erected for 400 or 500 people, which were mostly occupied by ladies. I should think there were from 2,000 to 3,000 people present. He spoke on the repeal of the Missouri compromise and of the steady and sure encroachment of slavery on the free territory, and it was considered as one of his ablest speeches. I got a front seat, for I was anxious to hear all he said, and as I sat there my mind went back twenty-five years, during the same month, when I met him in Springfield on the day of the big show, how he was dressed on that day and how he catechised me about coming through New Salem without having the mail opened—which I mentioned in a former article. In place of the short pants and brown linen coat and low shoes tied across the instep and buckeye hat, he wore a fine light linen suit, fine boots and a silk hat. Major Newton Walker and John Proctor accompanied him to the court house in a fine carriage, and I think Major Walker took him in his carriage the next day to Canton, where he was to speak again.

CHAPTER VIII.

SOME FACTS IN RELATION TO LINCOLN'S STOREKEEPING.—ERROR IN HERNDON'S BIOGRAPHY.—MR. LINCOLN A JUDGE IN HORSE-RACES.

When Mr. Lincoln ran for the legislature in 1832 and was defeated by Mr. Cartwright it was no disparagement to him, for Mr. Cartwright was one of the strongest and most popular men in the country, but it was a stimulus to greater activity by him, and it is probable that it was a providential thing that he was not elected, for he was only twenty-three years old and had never applied himself to that diligent study which prepared him for the great duties that he was afterwards called upon to perform. After his defeat he applied himself industriously to his books, so that in 1834, when he was two years older and considerable wiser, his friends brought him out again for representative. He was elected by a handsome majority and was re-elected in '36, '38 and '40, serving four terms, in all eight years, and in 1846 was elected to Congress.

I will now go back a little and state a few facts in regard to Mr. Lincoln's store-keeping, and how he became involved in a debt that hung over him for many years, for there have been many misstatements regarding it. When Mr. Lincoln kept the postoffice, the profits of the office did not afford him a fair living, and it confined him indoors so that he could not pursue any other occupation. There was a young man by the name of William Berry, who lived four miles from town with his father, Rev. John Berry, who was a Cumberland Presbyterian minister and a man of considerable property. William had attended the Jacksonville college and was a smart, intelligent young man, but inclined to be a little bit wild. His father, knowing the good habits of Mr. Lincoln, induced him to take William into partnership, and they purchased a store, paying a small part down and giving their notes for the balance. They kept the store in the same building with the postoffice and had as fair a trade, I think, as any of the other merchants in the town. The story told in W. H. Herndon's life of Lincoln, that after they had bought the first store they bought a second and then a third store on credit, and that Mr. Lincoln tried to get Berry to borrow money from his father to buy a fourth store, is all a fabrication. Mr. Lincoln was careful in all his dealings and was disposed to have too much confidence in men; being honest himself, he wanted to believe that other men were the same. He finally sold out his interest to his partner, who was to pay the debts. But young Berry soon after took to drinking, made some bad debts and took sick and died before the debt on the store was paid. It was the opinion of many persons at New Salem that the father of William Berry should have paid off the indebtedness and relinquished Mr. Lincoln, for it was through his influence that the boy had been taken as a partner. Mr. Lincoln was too honest to let the debt go, and, keeping the interest up, the first money he could save from his salary, when he was elected to Congress in 1846, he sent to his law partner, W. H. Herndon, to pay off the old debt.

Mr. Lincoln was very popular in and around New Salem, for in all his dealings he had been both honest and truthful, and had the respect of all who knew him, which was shown in his race for the legislature in 1832, when he received all but seven or eight of the 300 votes in his precinct.

New Salem, at the time Mr. Lincoln lived there, was a great place of resort for the young men to gather on Saturdays. The Clary Grove boys, the Island Grove boys, the Sangamon River boys and the Sand Ridge boys, each designated by the part of the country from which they came, would gather there to indulge in horse racing, foot racing, wrestling, jumping, ball playing and shooting at a mark. Mr. Lincoln would generally take a lay-off for part of the day and join in the sport. He was very stout and active and was a match for any of them. I do not think he bet on any of the games or races, but they had so much confidence in his honesty, and that he would see fair play, that he was often chosen as a judge to determine the winner, and his decisions were always regarded as just. He would generally speak on the subject of internal improvement and of the great resources of the State of Illinois, of its advantages over other states, and of the wonderful opportunities that lay in store for the young men of Illinois if they would only improve them. In those speeches he very seldom touched on politics, so everyone was pleased and none offended, the meeting generally closing with three cheers for Lincoln and a general handshaking. The people would go home happy, and few of them would come in town again until the next Saturday.

Mr. Lincoln was not only chosen as a judge in horse races, but was often the arbiter in disputes between his neighbors, and saved them many expensive law suits. A justice of the peace came into his office one day and complained that he had been cruelly wronged by him; that he had deprived him of many fine fees by interfering with his business. Mr. Lincoln replied that he could not bear to see his neighbors spend their money in litigation and become enemies for life when he could prevent it. When these cases were brought before him he would generally give satisfaction to both parties, and when one was in the wrong he would point out to him his error and convince him of it before he left.

CHAPTER IX.

SOME INCIDENTS OF W. H. HERNDON'S EARLY LIFE.—HIS FURTHER MISSTATEMENTS IN REGARD TO LINCOLN.

In writing of the early life of Abraham Lincoln, I think I had better give a sketch of the early life of William H. Herndon, who was for twenty years a law partner of Mr. Lincoln, and who wrote "Herndon's Life of Lincoln," contained in two volumes. There are but few persons now living who knew Mr. Herndon as well as I did in the days of his youth. He was a son of Archer G. Herndon, one of the early settlers of Springfield, who built and kept one of the first hotels ever erected in that city—the Herndon House. He was a prominent politician and had been elected State Senator, besides holding several other offices at different times. He was a Whig and a warm personal friend of Mr. Lincoln.

While I was carrying the mail I stopped two nights each week at the Herndon House, and there is where I became acquainted with William Herndon. We were about the same age, he being fourteen years old, while I was fifteen, and as we were both of a lively disposition and fond of sport, we spent a great deal of time together, commencing in the year 1832. He possessed one trait of character that many people objected to, and that was the delight he took in playing practical jokes. He did not seem to care how much misery and suffering he caused, so long as he had a little notoriety or fun out of it. In the fall of 1836 my father sent me to the Jacksonville college. A young man named Porter from Chicago was my room mate, but after I had been there about a week Bill Herndon came up to our room and told me that he had come to attend college and wanted to know if I would take him as a roommate, remarking that I was the only student with whom he was acquainted. I told him I was willing if Porter would consent, and Porter said he had no objections if I could furnish him bedding.

As I had a room to myself and a large bed, I took Herndon in and we bunked together. I noticed he had not brought a trunk with him, and I asked him where his trunk was. He said he had come away from home in a hurry and did not bring it, but that his folks would send it by the next stage. Then he commenced laughing, and I suspected he had been up to some of his old tricks, so I said: "Now, Bill, you have been in some devilment and you had to get away and you must tell us what it is." He said there had been an election for county officers up in Sangamon county and that one of the political parties had paid him $1.50 to take some tickets out to a precinct a few miles from Springfield and heel them among the voters. After he had gone a mile he was overtaken by a young man who had a package of tickets for the opposing party. The young man offered Herndon $1.50 to take his tickets and distribute them among the voters. Herndon accepted the offer and the first creek he came to he soused the tickets in, leaving the men who would have voted that ticket the alternative of writing their tickets or not voting. This act incited the wrath of the parties who had employed him first, so he had come away until the storm blew over. He told the story with such glee and merriment that it was evident he thought he had done something remarkably cute.

Herndon had not been at the college long until it was evident that he was brim full of devilment, and there was scarcely a week during the time he stayed there that he was not cited to appear before the faculty for some misdemeanor. It was not because there was anything bad about him that made him do as he did, but he wanted to gain notoriety and astonish somebody. After he left college he clerked in a store in Springfield for a long time, and then commenced the study of law. He applied himself to his studies, and was about twenty-five years old when he went in with Mr. Lincoln, who was nine years his senior. It was thought a little strange at that time that Mr. Lincoln would take into partnership so young and inexperienced a lawyer as Bill Herndon. But he had his reasons and I think I can come very near guessing some of them. Bill's father had been a friend to Lincoln for a great many years and was a very influential man in Sangamon county. He had always helped Lincoln in every way, and it was in payment for this kindness that Lincoln took his son in his office. It was a parallel case with that of Bill Berry, who Lincoln took in as a partner in his New Salem store. Both fathers wanted their sons in partnership with an honest man.

Then there was another reason. Both of Lincoln's partners, John T. Stuart and Stephen T. Logan, were, like himself, aspirants for political honors, and he had learned that a law office could not prosper when all the members of the firm wanted to be Congressmen. As Bill was young and showed no disposition to run into politics, he thought it was safe to take him into partnership. And Bill did apply himself to business, and, so far as I can learn, gave perfect satisfaction to the firm and to the people for whom he transacted business, up to the time of Lincoln's death. But for some unaccountable reason, after Mr. Lincoln died he commenced drinking. He had never drank before in his life, and moved out to his farm, seven miles east of Springfield, to get away from the saloons and his drinking companions.

I cannot but think that perhaps it was his ruling passion —to do something surprising—coupled with the habits of his later years, that induced him to make so many extravagant and untruthful statements in his "Life of Lincoln." I will mention a few of them. For instance, his statement that on his trip to New Orleans Lincoln bored a hole in the bottom of the flat boat to let the water out of course is untrue. He says Lincoln tried to drive some hogs onto the flatboat and when they would not go he sewed up their eyes so that they couldn't see where they were going, when the fact is there were no hogs taken on the boat, it being loaded with produce. He also says that Lincoln weighed 240 pounds when he lived in New Salem and could lift 1,000 pounds, and had been known to lift a barrel of whiskey by the chimes and drink out of the bung-hole; that after he bought the store in New Salem he bought a second, then a third, and tried to borrow money to buy the fourth, when not a dollar had been paid on any of them. The facts are Lincoln never weighed over 175 pounds in his life; was never known to take a drink of liquor out of anything, and never purchased but one store, and paid for that. Herndon also said that the mail was caried through New Salem in a four-horse coach, and that the postage on letters was five, ten, fifteen, twenty and twenty-five cents. The mail was carried on horseback and I rode the horse, and the postage on letters was $6\tfrac{1}{4}$, $12\tfrac{1}{2}$, $18\tfrac{3}{4}$ and 25 cents, according to the distance they were carried. He says the Rutledge tavern, where Lincoln boarded, was a one-story house with four rooms, when in fact it was a two-story eight-room house. I only make these statements to show that he knew nothing of what he was writing; that it was all guess work, and very poor guess work at that.

The cruelest and most outrageous statement, however, in Herndon's book is the story of Lincoln breaking his engagement to Miss Mary Todd. He say that on the 1st day of January, 1841, careful preparations had been made at the Edwards mansion for the wedding. The house underwent the customary renovation, the furniture was properly arranged, the rooms neatly decorated, the supper prepared and the guests invited. The latter assembled on the evening in question and waited in expectant pleasure the interesting ceremony of the marriage. The bride, bedecked in veil and silk gown, and nervously toying with the flowers in her hair, sat in the adjoining room. Nothing was lacking but the groom. For some strange reason he had been delayed. An hour passed and the guests, as well as the bride, were becoming restless. But they were all doomed to disappointment. Another hour passed and messengers were sent out over town, each returning with the same report. It became apparent that Lincoln, one of the principals in the little drama, had purposely failed to appear. The bride in grief dispersed the guests, who quietly and wonderingly withdrew; the lights in the Edwards mansion were blown out and darkness settled over all for the night. After daylight and after a persistent search Lincoln's friends found him. Restless, gloomy, miserable, desperate, he seemed an object of pity. His friends, fearing a tragic termination, watched him closely in their rooms day and night. Knives, razors and every instrument that could be used for self destruction were removed from his reach.

Now how any man can have the audacity to fabricate such a mass of falsehoods as the above story and put them in a book is beyond my comprehension. There is not a word of truth in it. Mr. Lincoln and Miss Todd were engaged at one time, but the wedding was put off one year by mutual consent, as Mr. Lincoln wanted to get his financial affairs in a little better condition before he took a wife.

CHAPTER X.

TRUE STORY OF THE LINCOLN-SHIELDS DUEL.

In giving a short historical sketch of the Lincoln-Shields duel, as some of the historians saw proper to call it, I will state a few facts and circumstances, as I understood them at the time, that induced Mr. Shields to challenge Mr. Lincoln to fight a duel.

William H. Herndon, in his history of the life of Lincoln, has appropriated some dozen pages in telling the story of that duel and has not told one-half of the difficulty that existed between Mr. Lincoln and Mr. Shields. He says the trouble grew out of an article that appeared in the Sangamon Journal, supposed to have been written by Mr. Lincoln, and which Mr. Shields considered derogatory to his character and standing as a state officer. But from all I could learn the green-eyed monster jealousy had more to do with Mr. Shields wanting to fight Mr. Lincoln than any thing else. Shields, Lincoln, Stephen A. Douglas and some other young lawyers about Springfield had been paying considerable attention to Miss Mary Todd, and Shields became deeply enamored with her. He had served a term in the legislature with a great deal of credit and was then holding the office of state auditor, and besides being an able lawyer he was quite popular in the democratic party. Miss Mary was a handsome, brilliant and highly-educated young lady, and there is no doubt that Shields wanted her to become his wife, but Mr. Lincoln was his rival, so when that article appeared in the Journal it gave him an excuse to challenge Lincoln to mortal combat.

According to the rules of dueling the person challenged chooses the weapons and fixes the distance the combatants are to stand apart. Mr. Lincoln took advantage of his rights as the challenged party and chose as the weapons broad swords of the largest size, precisely equal in every way, and such as were used by the cavalry at Jacksonville. A plank, ten feet long and from nine to twelve inches wide, was to be firmly fixed in the ground as the dividing line, over which neither was to pass his foot on forfeit of his life. Next two lines were to be drawn on the ground parallel with the board and the full length of the sword from the board, and if either party stepped over this line during the contest he would be counted as having been defeated. This scheme placed the parties about six feet apart, and gave Mr. Lincoln a tremendous advantage with his long legs and arms, while Shields was a short man with short arms and legs. The result would be that Lincoln by stooping over with his long arms could tickle Shields very uncomfortably about his ribs with the point of his sword, while Shields could not reach Lincoln by twelve or fifteen inches. It would have placed Shields completely at the mercy of Lincoln; but in all the world he could not have been in kinder hands, for it was never in Lincoln's big and tender heart to hurt a human being, except in self-defense.

But while the seconds and friends of the two parties were making preparations for the duel, John J. Hardin (one of the most influential men of the state, and a friend of both parties), having heard that they were going to fight a duel, hastened to the scene of action and declared that the thing had to stop, that there was nothing to fight about except a miserable little misunderstanding between them. Mr.

Hardin told the seconds to go to Shields and have him withdraw the offensive and threatening letter he had written to Lincoln, and then he believed Lincoln would give him a satisfactory explanation of the whole matter. Mr. Hardin's advice was taken, and then Mr. Lincoln explained that he had only written a short paragraph in The Journal which was not intended to reflect on Mr. Shields' character, but was merely an unmalicious electioneering document. Mr. Shields was satisfied with the explanation Mr. Lincoln gave, and the fight was declared off.

Now it is probable that there was not another man in Sangamon county at that time who, if he had received such a challenge, would not at once have made up his mind that he had to back down and confess that he was afraid to fight, or stand up and be shot at. But not so with Lincoln. With his great mind and head full of hard common sense he was able to solve all such questions and come out victorious with nobody hurt. Mr. Lincoln afterwards told his friends that he did not want to hurt Shields—that he had nothing against him; but if he had paid no attention to the challenge that Shields would have said he was a coward and had shown the white feather, and would have crowed over it like a bantam rooster, and he wanted to teach him to behave himself.

Herndon's Life of Lincoln says that Lincoln and Shields were to stand twelve feet apart in their duel; it is certainly an absurd mistake. At least I always understood that the distance was twice the length of one of the swords that were to be used. So I have no doubt that Mr. Herndon missed the mark six feet; but it was no uncommon thing for him to do. I find in his Life of Lincoln a great many instances in which he missed the mark more than six feet. For instance, he describes Mr. Shields at a hot-headed, blustering Irishman of but little prominence, when he was really a man of very great ability. He served as associate justice of the supreme court, was commissioner of the general land office, had the rare distinction of being at different times United States senator for three different states, and as a gallant officer of the Mexican War was advanced on his merits to the high place of major general.

After Mr. Lincoln was elected president he remembered his old friend that was a rival for his sweetheart and would have fought a duel for her hand, and showed his kind and forgiving spirit by presenting Shields with a brigadier general's commission. So Gen. James Shields must have been a man of considerable ability to have held these positions. He was a grand and patriotic man.

How wonderful was the wisdom and tact and sweetness of Lincoln in averting with honor to himself the duel that might have robbed our country of two such men!

CHAPTER XI.

MR. LINCOLN'S RELIGIOUS BELIEF.

Since I commenced writing these sketches of the earlier life of Mr. Lincoln I have sometimes been asked if I knew anything about his religious belief and how he stood with the orthodox world on that subject. I have never heard him express himself on that question, and I do not believe that he ever made a public profession of religion or connected himself with any church. But I know that he was looked upon as a moral and exemplary young man. I have understood that a minister remarked to him one day that he believed that he was a Christain man, and asked why it was that he did not join some church; and Mr. Lincoln is said to have replied that if he could find a church whose creed and requirements could be simmered down to the Savior's condensed statement, "Thou shalt love the Lord thy God with all thy heart, and with all thy soul, and with all thy mind, and thy neighbor as thyself," that he would join that church with all his heart and soul.

William H. Herndon in his Life of Lincoln has this to say of him:

"In 1834, while he lived in New Salem, and before he became a lawyer, he was surrounded by a class of people exceedingly liberal in matters of religion. Volney's Ruins and Paine's Age of Reason, and other infidel literature passed from hand to hand and furnished food for the evening in the tavern and village stores, and Lincoln read those books and thus assimilated them into his own being. He prepared an extensive essay, called by many a book, in which he made an argument against Christianity, striving to prove that the Bible was not inspired, and therefore not God's revelation, and that Jesus Christ was not the Son of God. The manuscript containing these audacious and comprehensive propositions he intended to have published or given a wide circulation in some other way. He carried it to the store where it was read and freely discussed. His friend and employer, Samuel Hill, was among the listeners, and seriously questioning the propriety of a promising young man like Lincoln fathering such unpopular notions, he snatched the manuscript from his hands and thrust it into the stove. The book went up in the flames, and Lincoln's political future was secured."

Now I have good reason to believe that Mr. Herndon drew largely on his imagination for this story. I believe it to be without foundation. As I have before stated, my business as mail carrier required me to be in Lincoln's store and postoffice a part of four days in each week to have the mail changed, and at the same time stopped at the same tavern with Mr. Lincoln. I generally kept my eyes and ears open and knew pretty well what was going on. If there had been any discussion or writing of the sort alluded to by Mr. Herndon I certainly would have known it. Mr. Herndon was then sixteen years old and lived at Springfield, twenty miles away. His father kept the hotel where I put up two nights out of each week, and I generally found Bill on hand either at the hotel or the stable. If he had been away from his business to visit New Salem to look up Mr. Lincoln's religious record, I think that I would have known something about it. It will be noticed that Mr. Herndon says that Mr. Hill threw the infidel document into the stove. Now I know very well that in 1834 Mr. Hill never had a stove in his store. I remember that in the Rutledge tavern, where Mr. Lincoln boarded, they had a shelf put up in the sitting room, and on this shelf the library was kept. There were some twenty five or thirty books—law books, histories and miscellaneous works—but none of those books referred to by Mr. Herndon.

I have always believed that from the first that I knew of Mr. Lincoln that he was a Christian and one of the best men that I ever knew. I think that all his acts, letters and public documents will show that Mr. Herndon was mistaken in regard to his infidelity.

In 1851 Mr. Lincoln learned that his father was not expected to live, and as he had sickness in his own family and could not go to see him, he wrote the following letter to his half-brother:

"I sincerely hope that father may yet recover his health; but at all events tell him to remember and call upon and confide in our great and good and merciful Maker who will not turn away from him in any extremity. He notices the fall of a sparrow, and numbers the hairs of our head, and he will not forget the dying man who puts his trust in him. Say to him that if we could meet now it is doubtful whether it would be more painful than pleasant; but if it be his lot to go now he will soon have a joyful meeting with the many loved ones gone before, and where the rest of us, through the help of God, hope ere long to join them."

It will be remembered that on his trip from Springfield to Washington to be inaugurated he addressed a multitude from the cars as he was leaving his old home and that among other things he spoke as follows:

"A duty devolves upon me which perhaps is greater than has devolved upon any other man since the days of Washington. He would have never succeeded except for the aid of Divine Providence upon which he had at all times relied. I feel that I cannot succeed without the same divine aid which sustained him, and in the same Almighty being I place my reliance for support, and I hope you, my friends, will all pray that I may receive that divine assistance without which I cannot succeed, but with which success is certain."

At another time when our armies were meeting reverses and the destiny of the nation seemed to be hanging in the balance, President Lincoln appointed a day for prayer for the success of the army in the following words:

"And, whereas, when our beloved country, once by the blessing of God united, prosperous and happy, is now afflicted with factions and civil wars, it is peculiarly fit for us to recognize the hand of God in this terrible visitation, and in sorrowful remembrance of our own faults and crimes as a nation and as individuals, to humble ourselves before Him and to pray for His mercy—to pray that we may be spared further punishment, though most justly deserved; that our armies may be blessed and made effectual for the re-establishment of law and order and peace throughout the wide extent of our country, and that the inestimable boon of civil and religious liberty, earned under His guidance and blessing by the labors and sufferings of our fathers, may be restored in all its original excellence. Therefore, I, Abraham Lincoln, President of the United States, do appoint the last Thursday in September next as a day of humiliation, prayer and fasting for all the people of the nation. And I do earnestly recommend to all the people, and especially to all ministers and teachers of religion of all denominations, and to all heads of families, to observe and keep that day according to their several creeds and modes of worship, in all humility, and with all religious solemnity, to the end that united prayers of the nation may ascend to the throne of grace and bring down plentiful blessing upon our country."

Now there is not much skeptical doctrines in these letters and utterances. So I think that we can claim that Mr. Lincoln was a pretty good orthodox Christian.

CHAPTER XII.

MY VISIT TO THE GRAVE OF THE MARTYRED PRESIDENT.

About three years after Mr. Lincoln had been buried at Springfield I went to that city to visit his resting place and to see my old college chum, William H. Herndon. I hoped we could go together to visit Lincoln's grave. But I found that Mr. Herndon had moved seven miles into the country, and that he had recently had a long and serious illness, so that he would probably not be able to come to the city at that time. I then learned for the first time of my old friend's dissipation, following Lincoln's death. At last his friends had to send him into the country to get him away from the saloons and his boon companions. No doubt, in his dissipated and mentally-wrecked condition, he had written the false and absurd things of Lincoln that marred his history of that great man—a history that contains much valuable truth and information. But his intemperate habits and abnormal mental condition are doubtless to blame for the absurd and silly stories that mar the history and wrong the memory of the good Lincoln. It is strange that men of good sense will reproduce these outrageous falsehoods in their papers and magazines as history, when there is neither truth nor history in them.

When I found that my unfortunate old school mate could not go with me, I went alone to Lincoln's grave. I was surprised to find that he was not buried in the old cemetery that I had often seen, but that his burial place was a long way north of town, and reached by street cars. When I got there I was again surprised to find his grave near the old stage road that ran in early times from Springfield to Peoria, and but a short distance from the old ferry where the road crossed the Sangamon river. All this ground was familiar to me. It brought to my mind many incidents of an historical nature. The ferry was of great importance in the olden times. The high land on either side came to the river, and it could therefore be crossed in any stage of water; but below this ferry for forty miles the river was difficult to cross, because of the low bottom lands that would overflow. Mr. Lincoln informed me of this fact, which he had discovered while navigating the river with flatboats and his steamboat. So it was that while I was carrying the mail in times of high water, instead of going from Athens to Sangamontown, and thus crossing deep sloughs and creeks, I kept up the river and crossed this ferry, two miles from Springfield, and so traveled up this old and familiar road that ran by Lincoln's grave.

Tradition tells us that it was at this ferry where Mr. Lincoln landed his canoe when he first came down the Sangamon river to make that locality his home, he then being a mere lad, and that he walked up the same old road to the hamlet of Springfield. It was at this ferry landing, also, that he landed and tied up for a week the steamboat Talisman, and stood upon her upper deck, and from day to day addressed the great crowds of people who flocked to the river to see the wonderful steamboat. These were the speeches in which he told the people of the wonderful possibilities of the great state, and of its opulent future, if these possibilities were improved. What a prophet he was! And yet he was in full view of the knoll on which was to stand his imperial monument of to-day, and never dreamed of the reverence and honor that would come to him. And I had often carried the mail over this ferry and highway close by this to be forever sacred spot, little thinking of the wonderful things to come in the following thirty-three years.

Mr. Lincoln's remains were then enclosed in a brick vault, the walls two feet thick and twelve feet high. Since then the great monument has been erected above his ashes.

I sat down by my old friend's grave while the old memories crowded thick and fast about me. I recalled my first acquaintance with him in 1832; the many times I sat at the same table with him at the Rutledge tavern in New Salem; of the many times we had joined in changing the mail; I remember the last time I traveled the road, carrying the pouch of letters his hands had touched; of the time he took the long walk in the hot sun to get Judge Thomas to fix the title papers to my land, refusing to accept a fee, because, he said, I had done favors for him. All of these incidents and numberless acts of kindness on his part crowded my memory. And then came before me his splendid future life with its mighty honors and mightier burdens; his election to the presidency; the long and terrible war in which he was the great commander of army and navy; that noble victory that under heaven he achieved, and his cruel death amidst the shouts for the union restored and peace assured forever. And sitting by his grave I paid the homage of tears to my boyhood friend, the best, and truest, and sweetest man I ever knew.

I believe that Lincoln might have said, the day before his assassination, as truly as did the Apostle Paul before his martyrdom:

"I have fought a good fight; I have finished my course; I have kept the faith; henceforth there is laid up for me a crown of righteousness, which the Lord, the Righteous Judge, shall give me at that day."

Andrew Jackson.

PERSONAL RECOLLECTIONS OF THE OLD HERO AND STATESMAN.

CHAPTER I.

THE CHURCHWELL AND KIRKPATRICK FAMILIES' PERSONAL ACQUAINTANCESHIP WITH THE OLD HERO AND STATESMAN.—HISTORY OF THE TRAGEDY IN WHICH ANDREW JACKSON PARTICIPATED.—OUR VISIT TO HIM AT THE HERMITAGE.—STORY OF MRS. JACKSON'S DEATH.—A LITTLE ANECDOTE ABOUT ALEXANDER KIRKPATRICK.

Since I closed the several sketches that I have been writing for The Fulton Democrat containing reminiscences of the lives of Abraham Lincoln and Peter Cartwright, I have received letters from Boston, Springfield and many other places requesting me to furnish them with copies of those letters. Some of the writers said they wished to write a history of the Life of Lincoln and wished to copy those letters into it. There have also been many requests that I should continue those sketches. But some of my children and grandchildren wish me to compile those letters in book form, and if I should do so I would like to write also a few sketches of what I knew and have been able to reliably learn of the life and character of Andrew Jackson, and add these to those already written of Lincoln and Cartwright.

I hope the readers will not think that I want to make myself conspicuous in writing up the history of great men, for I do not. But if I can tell some facts and give some new information that will be interesting and useful to my children, grandchildren and great-grandchildren, of which I have a pretty fair stock, and at the same time might interest other people, it would be all that I could desire.

Peculiar circumstances have given me the privilege of knowing a good many incidents relating to that grand hero and statesman, Gen. Jackson, that are not generally known. I remember very well the time that he ran for president in 1828, and many of the events connected with that very exciting campaign; and I visited him at the Hermitage and witnessed and enjoyed his kind and generous hospitality. I have also visited the memorable battle ground at New Orleans where the great battle was fought and won by Jackson and his men on the 8th of January, 1815, and procured some of the relics and trophies of that wonderful battle.

And now perhaps some of the readers may want to know how it happened that I, a resident of Illinois, ever came to know and learn very much about Andrew Jackson, who lived in Tennessee, and what led me to make him a visit at the Hermitage. So I will have to go into some family affairs to show how it happened. So I would say in the first place that all of my wife's relations back of the present generation were Tennesseans and were raised but a short distance from where Gen. Jackson lived, and they all knew him. My wife's father, Charles Kirkpatrick, who lived near Canton, Ill., and was an elder in the Presbyterian church of that place for many years, was a captain under Gen. Jackson in the war of 1812, and was with him in many expeditions against the Creek and Chickasaw Indians, and knew the old hero from his youth up. My wife's uncle (a brother to her mother), Col. George W. Churchwell, a prominent lawyer in that part of the country where General Jackson lived, had held the appointment of Indian agent under Jackson during a part of his presidential administration, and had practiced law at the bar with him, and had practiced law before the general when he was judge. Col. Churchwell's wife was also well acquainted with Jackson, and knew him at the time when he was converted and united with the Presbyterian church, and had sat at the communion table with him, herself being a Presbyterian. Now it was from these persons I got a good deal of my information about Gen. Jackson. Gen. Churchwell was widely known throughout that part of the country. In addition to his large law practice he was a farmer and breeder of fine stock. He had a farm of 500 acres two miles north of Knoxville, Tenn. At the time I visited him in 1843 he was the owner of some forty slaves of both sexes and all ages. Col. C. and wife came to Fulton county about every two years to visit his sister and family and to look after some lands he had there. It was on the occasion of one of those visits that I met with him and bargained for some of his fine stock. So in the fall of 1843 I started from Havana, Ill., with two horses and a carriage, in company with my wife's brother, Alexander Kirkpatrick, and my brother, Pike C. Ross, to go to Knoxville to bring home the stock. But before we started Captain Kirkpatrick charged us very particularly if we traveled near to the Hermitage to be sure to stop and see Gen. Jackson and to give to the old general his kind regards, and to tell him the number of his regiment and company, and what battles and expeditions they were in together.

I stated in my last communication that with my brother Pike C. Ross and my wife's brother, A. C. Kirkpatrick, I had made arrangements to go to Knoxville, Tennessee, to bring home some fine stock that I had purchased of my wife's uncle, Col. George W. Churchwell, who lived on a farm near that place. My brother Pike at that time was about eighteen years, and my wife's brother was two years older. Both were full of life and were desirous of getting as much pleasure out of the trip as possible.

We started from Havana, Mason county, about the first of October, 1843, with a span of fine traveling horses and a light carriage. Our route ran through a section of country where I had traveled as early as in 1829 and 30, and I could point out to the boys some of the old landmarks of that early day and tell them of the wonderful changes that had taken place in the country since I first traveled through it.

In 1828 when my father settled at Havana there was not a house on the Springfield road between Havana and Miller's Ferry on the Sangamon river, a distance of fifteen miles. And in all that section of country lying between the Sangamon river and the Mackinaw river and running east from the Illinois river for a distance of fifteen miles, containing at least 400 square miles, there was not a white inhabitant except three or four families at Havana. Great numbers of Indians lived along the water courses, and their Indian ponies by the thousands ranged over all that vast country.

As we traveled on we stopped at the old town of New Salem, Mr. Lincoln's old home and stamping ground, where he kept store and the post office. I had not been there since I carried the mail some ten years before, and I wanted to see how the old town looked. I found some of the old buildings still standing, but most of them had been taken to Petersburg. Mr. Lincoln's house, where he kept store and the post office, and Samuel Hill's store, where Mr. Lincoln had clerked, had been taken away. The old log tavern where Mr. Lincoln and I boarded was still there, and I wanted to patronize it for Auld Lang Syne's sake, but the old sign with "The New Salem Inn" on it had been taken down and we could get no accommodations. The frame of the water mill was still standing, but there was no longer a mill there. There is a little history about that mill and the men who built it which I will relate: It was at this mill that Mr. Lincoln first got employment when he came to New Salem, and it was at this mill that Samuel Hill had 100 barrels of flour made which Mr. Lincoln took to New Orleans on his flat boat. The mill was built by John Cameron and George Rutledge, who were also the proprietors of New Salem. John Cameron sold his interest in the mill and moved to Fulton county and settled on the bluffs half a mile south of where Bernadotte now stands. He was one of the proprietors of Bernadotte. He built a water mill at that place which was the first grist mill ever built on Spoon river. He moved from Fulton County to Oregon, and from there to California. He died in Oakland, California. His grandson, W. W. Cameron, represented Oakland in the state legislature, and was also mayor of Oakland.

The next place we came to that is worth mentioning was old Sangamontown, lying on the Sangamon river, and about eight miles from Springfield. It was laid out about the same time that Springfield was. It was at this place that Mr. Lincoln built the flat boat which he took to New Orleans, and it was at this place that Peter Cartwright organized his first church and Sabbath school after coming to Illinois. His residence was on a farm two miles south of the town.

We went on to Springfield and there took the old stage road that ran from Springfield to Vandalia. I remember traveling that road in 1829 in company with my father and a hired man. We were taking a drove of horses from Havana to St. Louis for sale, as that place was at that time the principal market for all Illinois. There was not a house or habitation from Springfield to Macoupin, a distance of eighteen miles. The whole country was covered with high grass, in many places extending above the backs of our horses. And then there was another thing that happened to us that I will never forget. It was the terrible fight we had with the horseflies. It appeared as if that whole country was swarming with horseflies. There was the small fly that would cover the head and ears of the horses, the green-headed and large black fly. They would torment the poor horses so that they would run into the high grass and roll over to get rid of them. Sometimes a half dozen would be down at once. We had hard work to keep the horses we rode from doing the same thing. When we got to Macoupin Point we were told that our trip across the prairie ought to have been made in the night, that during the summer season the stages and most all travelers crossed the prairie at night to avoid the flies.

When we left Sangamon we struck through for Vandalia, where the capital of the state had been located for many years before it was removed to Springfield. I had a strong desire to visit the old town of Vandalia that I had heard so much talk about. For a number of years after the settlement of the country all the land in the state owned by individuals upon which the taxes had not been paid were sold for the taxes at Vandalia. I remember that my father and Joel Wright of Canton and a few other men of Fulton county were in the habit of going to Vandalia to attend these sales. My brother Lewis lived at Vandalia at one time about a year. It was in 1828 or '29. He went there to learn the printer's trade. He held the position I think of what that craft calls the "printer's devil." He worked for Judge James Hall, who was one of the first editors in the state. I think he moved out of the state and my brother gave up the trade. It was at Vandalia where Mr. Lincoln first went to the legislature, and Major Newton Walker was a member at the same time from Fulton county.

From Vandalia we traveled southeast to the Ohio river. We found the country from Vandalia to the river settled generally by people who emigrated from the slave-holding states, and the improvements were much inferior to the country we had passed between Springfield and Vandalia. Where the country had been settled mostly by eastern people in the southern part of the state a great many people were still living in their log houses, and small farms in cultivation; part of their land was planted in tobacco, cotton and flax. The southern counties had been settled much longer than the northern and middle counties, but were far behind in improvements. I will mention a little circumstance that happened as we were traveling through that part of the country, which was a little amusing to my young companions, and will demonstrate the amount of enterprise the people possessed: We stopped one day at a farm house to get a drink of water, and the lady of the house came out with a gourd that would hold a half gallon and told us that if we wanted a good cool drink that we had better go to the well, and pointed to where it was, and remarked that if we found any polliwigs in the water we were to pound the gourd against the side of the ladder that was in the well and they would all go to the bottom. So my brother Pike climbed down the well on the ladder and found the water alive with polliwigs, but he obeyed instructions and pounded the gourd against the side of the ladder and the polliwigs all disappeared and he brought up the gourd full of water without a polliwig or a tadpole in it.

We went on the Ohio river and was informed that the best way to go Knoxville in Tennessee was to go through Nashville. So when we got to Nashville we put up at the City Hotel, which we found afterwards was the very hotel where the wonderful tragedy had taken place between General Jackson and the Bentons, where Jackson, in attempting to horsewhip Thomas H. Benton, was shot by Jesse Benton, a brother of Thomas, putting a ball through his arm and one in his shoulder. The particulars of the fight and the cause of it I will give further on.

On our arrival at Nashville, as stated last week, we put up at the City Hotel, where the terrible tragedy had taken place between General Jackson and the two Bentons. The landlord had kept the hotel for a good many years, and was well acquainted with Gen. Jackson. There were also several men staying at the hotel who had been personally acquainted with Gen. Jackson for twenty or thirty years, and they gave us a good deal of information about him and the circumstances of the fight, as follows:

Thomas H. Benton, the old United States senator, who, I believe, served longer in the senate than any other man, had a brother Jesse who lived in Nashville, and who had got into some trouble with another Nashville man named Wm. Carroll. Jesse Benton sent Carroll a challenge to fight, and he accepted the challenge. Carroll and Jackson were warm friends, he having served under Jackson in the army as captain. So he went out to the Hermitage to see if Jackson would act as his second in the duel, but Jackson objected, saying that he was a friend of the Bentons and he did not want to do anything that would offend them. But he told Carroll that he would go to Nashville and see Jesse Benton and try to have the matter settled between them without any fighting, and he came to town and tried to have the matter settled between them. But Benton gave him to understand that Capt. Carroll would have to fight or show the white feather, saying that he would run him out of town. Benton made use of some language that Jackson thought was rather insulting, and so he consented to act as Carroll's second in the duel. They went out and took a crack at each other. Benton was wounded quite severely in the side, though not dangerously, and Capt. Carroll was slightly wounded in the left thumb. Benton was laid up twenty days with his wound. Thomas H. Benton, the brother of Jesse, was in Washington city at the time of the duel. When he received the news that his brother Jesse had fought a duel with Capt. Carroll and was badly wounded, and that Carroll had but a slight wound in his left thumb, and that General Jackson had been a second to his brother's antagonist, his wrath and indignation knew no bounds, and not having the facts in the case, he wrote Jackson very insulting and abusive letters, accusing him of all kinds of treachery and dishonesty, and some of his letters were published in the Nashville papers. These things aroused all the old tiger there was in Gen. Jackson, and while his wrath and high temper had the control of his better judgment he made a solemn vow in the presence of some of his friends that. "By the eternal, the first time I get my eyes on Tom Benton I will horsewhip him!" So in about a month after the duel was fought Thomas H. Benton came to Nashville and put up at the City Hotel. His brother Jesse by that time had recovered from his wound so that he was able to walk about the streets. In a few days after, Gen. Jackson rode to town to get his mail, left his horse at the Nashville Inn, but kept his horsewhip in his hand. After he got his mail he walked past the City Hotel and there observed Thomas H. Benton and his brother Jesse standing in front of the hotel a-talking He walked up to Benton and told him that he had to take back those scandalous assertions that he had made about him or he would have to take a horsewhipping. At that Benton made some pretense as if he were going to draw a pistol. Then Jackson drew his revolver and told him that if he attempted to draw a weapon he would get the contents of his pistol. Jesse Benton, who was standing near, seeing the predicament that his brother was in and with little chance to defend himself, drew his pistol and blazed away at Jackson and brought him to the ground, pistol, horsewhip and all. His pistol was loaded with two balls, one of which went through Jackson's arm and the other lodged in his shoulder. Jackson carried that ball in his shoulder for twenty years. The fight created a wonderful excitement in Nashville. The news ran like wildfire, and in ten minutes after Jackson was shot a thousand men were at the hotel and many fights took place between the friends of the two parties. One of Jackson's friends knocked Jesse Benton down and pounded him almost to death. Thos. H. Benton in the fight and skirmishing fell through an open doorway into the basement of the hotel, which saved him from getting a terrible whipping. The landlord told us that Jackson was confined at the hotel about three weeks before he could be removed to his home.

Soon after this occurrence Thos. H. Benton left the state of Tennessee and moved to Missouri, and he and Jackson did not meet again until sixteen years after, when they met as senators in Washington and had selected seats, unknown to either of them, that were located side by side; and they were both placed on some important committee, so that they had to come face to face. But they at once shook hands and were forever after good friends.

The next morning we started on our way to the Hermitage, which was some ten or eleven miles from Nashville. We traveled on a fine turnpike road which ran through a fertile country. On the road between Nashville and the Hermitage we passed the spot where there had been built at one time a fort or blockhouse, where the people gathered when the Indians were troublesome.

This fort, we were told, was afterwards purchased by Gen. Jackson and a man named Coffee and converted into a storehouse, and there they kept store for some years under the name of Jackson & Coffee. They bought large quantities of cotton and produce and shipped it down the Cumberland and Mississippi rivers in flatboats to New Orleans. Near the fort was one of the finest racetracks in the state, and there they also had a place erected for the exhibition of game cocks, where people came from hundreds of miles and from other states with their race horses and game cocks. Thousands of dollars would be bet on the races and cock fights.

We found the Hermitage was located about a half a mile from the turnpike road that ran from Nashville to Knoxville, but he had a private road that ran from the turnpike up to his house. Before we got to his house we passed a small brick Presbyterian church which we were told that Gen. Jackson had built on his own land for the accommodation of his wife after she united with that church; and it was at this little church where he was converted and joined the Presbyterian church, of which I may have something more to say. We drove up to the house and hitched our horses, opened the little iron gate and went in. We found the general sitting on his front piazza reading a newspaper. We introduced ourselves to him as well as we could, and told him we were from Illinois and on our way to Knoxville to take home some fine stock that I had purchased from Col. George W. Churchwell of that place, and told him of our relationship to Capt. Charles Kirkpatrick, who had served under him, and gave him the number of the regiment and the company that he commanded. The general said he remembered him very well, and told us of several expeditions they had been on together, and appeared to be pleased that we had called to see him, and asked us to have our horses put up and stay to dinner with him. But I told him as it was early in the day we would rather drive a few miles further before dinner. He said he was always glad to hear from any of the old comrades who were with him in the army, and was glad to meet any of their relatives. He asked my brother-in-law a good many questions about his father; wanted to know in what part of Illinois he lived, what his occupation was, and how many children he had. He said he knew his father very well, and also his two brothers then living in Tennessee. He also said he was very well acquainted with his uncle, George W. Churchwell, who had held the office of Indian agent when he was president, and had practiced law before him when he was judge. He also said that he knew his aunt, Col. Churchwell's wife; that they were both Presbyterians. He asked us if we would take a walk with him out in his orchard, saying he had some pretty good eating apples. But before we went to the orchard he took us through several rooms of his house. In one room he had a large library of books, with a number of fine pictures hanging around the walls. In another room he had a great lot of old war relics, such as old swords, pistols and old muskets, all with flint locks, and a great lot of old regimental clothing that was hanging around the walls. Some of it looked like it might have been worn in the times of the Revolutionary War. The Hermitage was a good, substantial building, but everything about it was very plain. Such a house could have been built in Illinois at that time for $4,000. He told me that his wife's nephew, Mr. Donelson and family, were living with him. He took us to his barn and showed us a span of carriage horses that he had, but they were not as good as the span I was driving. His barn was quite plain—no better than many Illinois farmers had at that time. We went from the barn to the orchard. He had a very fine orchard and a most excellent quality of fruit. He told us to tie up in our handkerchiefs and take all the apples we wanted to eat on our way. So we laid in a pretty fair supply which lasted till we got across the mountains. I told the general that he had some good eating apples and that I would like to take a half dozen home to my wife and boy; that I had a boy sixteen months old, and I could tell them when I got home that the apples came from Gen. Jackson's orchard. So he took me to a tree of large red apples which he called winesaps; so I gathered the apples and stored them away carefully in my satchel and brought them home. As we were returning from the orchard to the house he took us through a lot that lay a few rods east of the house and there showed us the grave of his wife. It was a plat of ground about 8x10 feet, enclosed with a marble wall rising about three feet above the ground, and a partition wall in the middle; on one side his wife was laid and was covered with a marble slab on which was engraved, " Mrs. Rachel Jackson, died 23rd December, 1828, aged sixty-one years." The general told us that when he died that he expected to be laid by his wife in the enclosed plat of ground. He spoke of his poor health and said that he did not think it would be many months until he would be lying there. He was very thin in flesh and pale at that time. He had us come into the the house again and brought in a pitcher of cold water. I asked him if he had ever been in Illinois. He said he had not, but he had become acquainted with a good many Illinois men when he was in Congress and while he was president, and named over several that I knew. He also said that he had been acquainted with a Methodist preacher who had been a delegate to the Nashville conference by the name of Peter Cartwright, who was now living in Illinois, and asked me if I knew him. I told him that I knew him very well; that he had often staid at my father's house and had preached in our log cabin in the early pioneer times, before there were any church buildings put up. He then went on and told the story that when Cartwright was preaching one time in Nashville he went to hear him, and as he was walking down the aisle the preacher in the pulpit by the side of Cartwright gave his coat a jerk and told him that Gen. Jackson was coming in; at which Cartwright spoke out so loud that all the church could hear him:

"Who is Gen. Jackson? If he don't get his soul converted God will damn him as quick as He would a Guinea negro!" I suppose the general thought I had never heard the story; but I heard it some years before from the Cartwright side, and was pleased to hear it from the other side.

The general went down to the carriage with us to see our horses, and admired them very much, for they were splendid animals. He told us to give his kind regards to Col. Churchwell and wife when we got to Knoxville, and also to Capt. Charles Kirkpatrick when we got home.

There was one circumstance which I omitted to mention relating to my visit to the Hermitage, which was the splendid arrangement which Jackson had made for the pleasure and good of his slaves. Each family had a one-story frame house that was painted either white or red, and with it about an acre of ground, all fenced in with palings or board fence and whitewashed; and around each of these houses were a lot of fruit trees and shrubbery. We were told that the general was always good and kind to his slaves, and would never permit any of them to be sold to go to the southern states, and that his slaves were strongly attached to him, and that nothing would induce them to leave their old master. Notwithstanding the terrible temper that the general possessed, which made him like a Kansas cyclone when he was imposed upon and aroused, he still possessed a kind and tender heart. Many people told us, who had known the general and his good wife during all their thirty-seven years of married life, that she was a grand and noble Christian lady, and was honored and loved by everybody; that their affection for each other was of the tenderest kind; that the general always treated her as if she was his pride and glory, and that words could faintly describe her devotion to him; that it was seldom that a husband and wife lived as happily together as they had done. We were told that when Mrs. Jackson died no such demonstration had ever been known at a funeral in that part of the country before; that the mayor of Nashville issued a proclamation requesting business men to close their stores and asked that the bells of the city be tolled from 1 to 2 P. M., during the funeral. Every vehicle in the city was employed in taking people to the Hermitage, where the funeral was held. It was estimated that 10,000 people attended the funeral. The death of

Mrs. Jackson was a terrible shock to the general, and some of his slaves went almost frantic with grief and despair. Such weeping and wailing had never been heard at a funeral, nor so much affection shown by slaves on the death of a mistress.

There was a little circumstance that took place in connection with the life of Gen. Jackson that I thought I would mention. I heard my father-in-law, Capt. Charles Kirkpatrick, speak of it, and also his brothers and some others that we met on our visit to Tennessee. It was on one of Gen. Jackson's expeditions against the Cherokee Indians, and will show that he did possess a kind and tender heart. The general and his soldiers were pursuing a band of Indians, and surrounded them; and as the Indians were attempting to escape every one was killed. In going to their wigwams they discovered a little boy papoose, and as the soldiers were about to dispatch him, the general commanded them not to hurt the little boy. And he took the little Indian boy home with him, and raised him, and sent him to school, and became very much attached to him. The little Indian boy became very expert in the riding of racehorses. He could get more speed out of them than any rider in the country; as the general was keeping some racehorses at the time, the boy made himself quite useful to the general. When the boy got to be fifteen years old the general thought he had better learn a trade; so he took him around among the artisans and mechanics in Nashville to choose the trade that he would prefer; so he chose the trade of saddlery and harness-maker, but after working at it a year he died. It was thought that if he had lived that the general would have made provisions for him in his will.

In giving this story about Gen. Jackson and the little Indian boy I might with some propriety make use of a habit peculiar to Mr. Lincoln; after listening to a story told by a friend, he would say: "Now, that puts me in mind of a little anecdote," and would go on and relate one of his quaint and humorous stories to match the one told him. So the circumstance about Gen. Jackson and the Indian boy has brought to my mind a similar circumstance that took place with Alexander Kirkpatrick, who was with me at the time we visited Gen. Jackson. Whether the story above told about Jackson and the Indian boy had any bearing on the story that I am about to tell I cannot say.

Alexander Kirkpatrick, in 1847, went to study medicine with Dr. W. H. Nance, at Vermont, Illinois, and in 1850 went to California, and practiced medicine in San Francisco and also in Redwood City. He became very eminent in his profession, having at one time the largest practice in San Francisco. In 1861 there was ordered out in California a regiment of soldiers to go into the northern border of the state to fight the Indians, who had been murdering a good many families. Dr. Kirkpatrick got the appointment of surgeon to go with the army. On that expedition they came upon the camp of the hostile Indians and surrounded them, and as they attempted to escape everyone was killed. The soldiers went inside of the wigwams and there found a little girl papoose. One of the soldiers was about to run his bayonet through her when Dr. Kirkpatrick jumped in before him and caught the little girl up in his arms and saved her life. Some of the soldiers who had lost relatives by the Indians were determined that she should share their fate; but the doctor drew his revolver and said that he would protect the girl at the risk of his life. He brought the little Indian papoose home and raised and educated her the same as he did his own children. The doctor told me that the child had so many droll and quaint ways about her and was so different from other children that he gave her the name of "Topsy," after the girl spoken of by Harriet Beecher Stowe in "Uncle Tom's Cabin." So she always went by the name of Topsy Kirkpatrick up to the time of her marriage with a white man. I have asked the doctor if he thought that the stories we heard in Tennessee about Jackson and the Indian boy had anything to do with his rescue of the Indian girl, and he said he thought that it had.

Dr. Kirkpatrick died in San Francisco in 1894, leaving a widow and two sons and three daughters and Topsy to mourn his loss. He was a kind-hearted, noble and generous man, and was loved and honored by all who knew him. He left a beautiful home to his family and life insurance to the amount of $20,000.

CHAPTER II.

BRIEF HISTORY OF PRESIDENTIAL ELECTION OF 1828.—SOME FURTHER INCIDENTS CONCERNING JACKSON.—OUR DELIGHTFUL VISIT IN THE SOUTH.—HOW MY SON FRANK* FINALLY CAME TO PARTAKE OF SOUTHERN HOSPITALITY AT THE HANDS OF "AUNT MOODY."—DEATH OF ANDREW JACKSON SHORTLY AFTER OUR RETURN FROM THE SOUTH.

I will give a little history of the presidential election of 1828, when Andrew Jackson ran against John Quincy Adams. At that time I was about twelve years old, and very distinctly remember the election held in Lewistown, Illinois. It was probably the most exciting election, and probably more bitter feeling indulged in, than at any election that has ever taken place in this country. For several months before the election almost every occupation was dropped and the men occupied their time electioneering. Almost every day long lines of men could be seen marching after the fife and drum and led by some officer that had served in the war of 1812. The Jackson party would erect their hickory poles and the Adams party their tall maple poles, and stands would be erected under their respective poles, and the best speakers in the country would be brought out, and each party would have a barbecue of a roast ox or half-a-dozen sheep about every week. At that time a good many who belonged to their respective parties had been soldiers in the war of 1812, and on their march would wear

---

* Now the Hon. Frank W. Ross, of Salt Lake City, Utah. He was the youngest elective officer—being a Lieutenant at the age of fifteen—in the Federal Army, and served with great bravery and distinction in all the battles of his regiment during the entire war, from '61 to '65.—C. K. O.

their soldier's uniform which they wore in the army. My
father had served as major under Gen. Brown, of New
York. I can remember very well how he looked, dressed
in his military suit, with his sword buckled on and hanging
by his side, wearing his soldier hat decorated with a large
cockade on one side of his hat and with two feather plumes
extending eight or ten inches above the crown of his hat,
decked off with the red, white and blue—all showing the
rank he held in the army. He rode a large white horse,
with a pistol holster swung across the pommel of his saddle,
in which were two large horse-pistols with their flint-locks.
So in marching in parade after the fife and drum he made
a pretty fair military appearance.

The election in Lewistown at that time was held at the
log court house. They had no such thing in that part of
the county at that time as saloons; but the candidates and
their friends had a different method of treating their
friends and voters if they wished to have something to
drink. A platform was erected some thirty feet long in
front of the court house, upon which was placed barrels,
kegs, demijohns and jugs, and the names of the candidates
written on their respective vessels. I remember that the first
vessel that was placed upon the platform was a thirty-gallon
barrel of whisky, with the name of " ANDREW JACKSON "
written upon it; and in a short time another barrel of the
same size was placed by its side, with the name of " JOHN
QUINCY ADAMS " written upon it in large letters. Then
came the ten and five-gallon kegs; then the demijohns and
jugs, with the names of the candidates who had bought the
liquor, and everybody was welcome to all they wished to
drink. At that time whisky was selling at thirty-five cents
a gallon by the barrel, or fifty cents a gallon at retail; and it
was a marvelous fact that after the election was over scarcely
any person had been intoxicated during the day. At that
time ballots were not used as at the present time, but each
voter, after his name was registered, would call out the
names of the candidates, one at a time, that he wished to
vote for. There were no national issues at that time to
divide the two parties, but each man ran on his own per-

sonal popularity. The campaign was carried on with a great deal of severity and bitterness. Adams was accused of corruption and extravagance in his former administration, and of being proud and selfish, and of being no friend of the poor and of the laboring man. On the other side Jackson was accused of every crime and offense and impropriety that ever a man was known to be guilty of. The most was made of his many duels, and hand-bills were issued and sent broadcast over the country telling of his cruelty and bad character. An account was given of the six men he had ordered to be shot in the army for mutiny and desertion, and their coffins were pictured out on the handbills. But the most cruel and malicious stories that were told about him were that he and his wife had lived together in open adultery before they were married. This story aroused more anger and bitter feeling against the Adams party than any other thing that had been told, for it was a falsehood, and his friends sternly resented that slander. Many a hard fist-fight took place between the friends of the two parties in consequence of that story.

I was told at the time when I traveled through Tennessee, in 1843, and by persons who had known Mrs. Rachel Jackson from the time that she was fifteen years old up to the time of her death, that there had never lived in the state of Tennessee a lady that stood higher or was more respected than Mrs. Jackson; that she was a pure and kind-hearted Christian lady. Those infamous falsehoods published about Gen. Jackson and his wife did more to arouse the indignation of the whole state of Tennessee against Adams and in support of Jackson than anything else. When the election came off there was less than 3,000 votes cast for Mr. Adams in that state. Some of the towns cast their entire vote for Jackson. I was told a story of how a stranger had come into one of the towns about election time and put up at the hotel and took a walk through the town. He found a great many women on the streets, but scarcely a man could be seen. He came back to the hotel and enquired of the landlord why it was that so many women were seen on the streets and no men; and the landlord told him that the men had gone out of town to hunt a couple of criminals, and when the stranger wanted to know what great crime these two men had committed that the whole town had gone in pursuit of them, the landlord told him they had voted for Mr. Adams! The people had been anxious to carry the place unanimously for Jackson, as many of the other towns had done, and the two rascals had spoiled the record, and the people were so indignant that they were hunting them so that they could tar and feather them, and the women were waiting on the streets anxious to see it done. But the men escaped to the woods and could not be found.

It was a fact that Mrs. Rachel Jackson was married three times—once to Lewis Roberts and twice to Gen. Jackson. The peculiar circumstances of her marriage to Gen. Jackson caused a good deal of gossip. But when the circumstances were understood there was nothing wrong about it, as I can show as I proceed with the narrative.

I can remember the men who took an active part in the politics of Fulton county in the election of 1828, and will give the names of a few of the leaders. On the side of Mr. Adams there were Stephen Phelps and his sons Alexis, Myron, Sumner and William; also Wm. Proctor, Joel Wright, Stephen Dewey, Peter Wood, Ossian M. Ross and his brothers, Joseph, Thomas and John; Hugh R. Coulter, John McNeil and David W. Barnes. On the Jackson side were William Walters (the hero of Rev. Wm. J. Rutledge's letters) and his brothers Daniel, Thomas and John, and an uncle, Abner Walters; the Waughtels, John and William Totten, and John Barker. The Adams men were generally from the East and the Jackson men from the Southern states. There are only four of the men and boys I knew at that time who are now living, viz: Mason Eveland and Henry Warren, of Iowa, Henry Andrews, of Canton, and my brother, Leonard F. Ross, of Lewistown.

In continuing my narrative of the trip I took through Tennessee at the time I visited Gen. Jackson I may allude to incidents that will not greatly interest the general reader. But it will be remembered that I am writing these sketches chiefly for the benefit of my children, grandchildren and great-grandchildren, so the reader will pardon these departures from the main theme of these sketches.

So I will take up our line of travel from the time we bade Gen. Jackson goodby at the Hermitage and turned our horses' heads towards Knoxville. The first place we stopped at was Lebanon. I have read somewhere in divine history something about the cedars of Lebanon, and when we drove into town we began to think we had found that place. Lebanon contained about 1,000 inhabitants, and was built in the middle of a large cedar grove. Part of the houses were built of logs and part were frame. The logs were all cedar and the frame houses were all built of cedar; the roofs were covered with cedar shingles and the fences and gates were all of cedar. So we concluded that Lebanon was a very appropriate name for the town.

We stopped over night at a hotel on the top of the Cumberland mountains. I went out to the barn after supper to see how our horses had been cared for. This was my custom, as we had a long journey to make and a good deal depended upon the condition of our team. I asked the negro hostler how much corn he had fed the horses. He said he had given them six ears apiece. I told him that he should have fed them twice that amount, but he answered, "Massa, they are great big ears." I asked how large the ears were. He said that they were almost as long as his arm and as big around as his leg. Then I said I wanted to see some of that corn; so he took me to the crib and I saw that the negro was not far out of the way, for they were the most wonderful ears of corn in size that I had ever seen. There was about as much feed in one ear as in two ears of common corn. I asked the landlord how it was that such large corn would grow on top of the Cumberland mountains. He said that there was a dark sandy loam on the mountains—just the kind of soil to produce large corn. So I went to the crib and selected one of the largest ears I could find, and shelled it, and packed it away in my satchel, intending to bring it home and try it on our Illinois soil, as I was at that time carrying on a large farm a half mile east of Havana in Mason county. I planted the corn by itself so that it would not get mixed with the other corn, and from that planting I raised several bushels. The next year I planted part of it and distributed the balance among some of my neighbor farmers, as I wanted to have it introduced all over the county. They gave it the name of the "Tennessee Mammoth Corn." I am sure that after I commenced raising that corn that the yield to the acre was at least a third more than it had been with common corn. Afterwards many Fulton county farmers came over to Mason county to get their seed corn.

We finally arrived at Col. Churchwell's with everything in good trim. Our horses had stood the trip excellently. Col. Churchwell and wife and about half a dozen negro servants were ready to meet us as they had heard that we were coming. We still had on hand some of the apples that Gen. Jackson had given us and we distributed them among the colonel's family and the servants, as they all wanted to taste the apples because they had come from Gen. Jackson's orchard. We delivered the messages the general had sent to Col. Churchwell and wife, and that led them both to tell us some marvelous stories about the general, for they had known him most all their lives. The colonel told us of a time that he was attending court in a neighboring town and Gen. Jackson was the presiding judge. A certain man had committed a crime, and a warrant had been placed in the hands of the sheriff, and he had summoned a half dozen men to assist him in making the arrest, for the man was a desperate character and was armed with several pistols and a bowie knife. The sheriff came into court and reported to the judge that the man could not be taken—that he and his men could not afford to risk their lives with such a character. The judge then said to him, "Summons Andrew Jackson to assist in taking that man." The sheriff did so, and Jackson took his hat and walked out of the court house and across the street to where the man was surrounded by many friends. Judge Jackson walked up to him, put his hand on his shoulder, and said to him, "You are my prisoner; you must go with me to the court house." The man made no resistance but walked deliberately to the court house where the judge took the pistols and knife from him and handed them to the sheriff. The man was asked afterwards why he did not resist Gen. Jackson as he had done the other men. He said he could see fight in the eyes of the judge, but could not see it in the eyes of the other men.

Col. Churchwell's wife could also tell us of many circumstances connected with the life of the general. She told us about what a time the minister had had with him to get him to agree to forgive his enemies when he was about to join the church. He told the minister that he was willing to forgive all his political enemies, but his enemies that had been guilty of defaming his private character and his wife, and of lying about his mother, he did not think he could forgive. But the minister told him that if he expected to have his sins forgiven he would have to forgive his enemies, and pointed him to many passages of scripture that treated on that subject. So the general finally agreed to forgive his enemies and was received as a member of the Presbyterian church. It took place at the little brick church near the Hermitage that he had built for his wife soon after they were married. I was told that Jackson and his wife were regular attendants at church while she was living, and that he was always a friend to all religious institutions, and that all his ancestors, including his mother, were Presbyterians. I will quote a few sentences from the biography of Peter Cartwright to show what the old pioneer Methodist preacher had to say about him, as follows:

"Gen. Jackson was certainly a very extraordinary man. He was no doubt in his prime of life a very wicked man, but he always showed a great respect for the Christian religion and the feelings of religious people, especially ministers of the gospel. I will here relate a little incident that shows his respect for religion. I had preached one Sabbath near the Hermitage, and in company with several gentlemen and ladies went by special invitation to dine with the general. Among the company there was a young sprig of a lawyer from Nashville, of very ordinary intellect, and was trying very hard to make an infidel of himself. As I was the only preacher present the young lawyer kept pushing his conversation on me in order to get into an argument. I tried to evade an argument, in the first place considering it a breach of good manners to interrupt the social conversation of the company, and, in the second place, I plainly saw that his head was much softer than his heart, and that there were no laurels to be won by vanquishing or demolishing such a combatant; I persisted in evading an argument. This seemed to inspire the young man with more confidence in himself, for my evasiveness he construed into fear. I saw Gen. Jackson's eyes strike fire as he sat by and heard the thrusts made at the Christian religion. At length the young lawyer asked me this question:

"'Mr. Cartwright, do you believe there is any such place as hell?'

"'Yes, sir; I do.'

"To which he responded:

"'Well, I thank God I have too much good sense to believe any such thing.'

"I was pondering in my mind whether I would answer him or not when Gen. Jackson for the first time broke into the conversation, and, directing his words to the young man, said with great earnestness:

"'Well, sir, I thank God that there is such a place of torment as hell.'

"This sudden answer, made with great earnestness, seemed to astonish the youngster, and he exclaimed:

"'Why, Gen. Jackson, what do you want of such a place of torment as hell?'

"To which the general replied, as quick as lightning:

"'To put such a rascal as you in that opposes and villifies the Christian religion!'"

After a cordial welcome to myself and my two young

comrades we had a delightful time going with Col. Churchwell over his splendid farm of 500 acres, located two miles north of Knoxville, Tennessee. His negroes cultivated about 300 acres, and the balance was in timber and seeded down to blue grass. He was engaged in raising fine-blooded stock. He had a fine dwelling house and ten or twelve frame houses on his place that his slave families occupied. He had fine barns and stables, and all his buildings and improvements were very good. He had about forty slaves of both sexes and of all ages. He was good and humane to his slaves and would never permit any of them to be sold to go to the southern plantations. His nephew was his overseer, and he told me that he very seldom had to punish a slave. Col. Churchwell was a member of the Methodist church, and his wife was a Presbyterian. It was his habit to hold family prayers morning and evening and he asked a blessing at his table. He and his wife were regular attendants at church. Sometimes both would go to the Methodist church and then to the Presbyterian church. Many of the slaves were church members, some belonging to one church and some to the other. Both Col. Churchwell and his wife believed that slavery was a divine institution, and that there was no harm in owning slaves, and the only harm there was about it was the abuse sometimes shown them by their masters. There was a very radical difference of opinion among my wife's relatives in regard to slavery, for on her father's side I have never known any of them to buy or sell a slave, although many of them were able to do so; but on her mother's (Churchwell's) side I never knew any of them who would not buy slaves if they had the money to do so.

The colonel and his good wife, "Aunt Moody," as we called her, did everything in their power to make us have a good and happy time. Their southern hospitality was manifested in many ways.

As stated in my first letter, the colonel and his wife were in the habit of visiting relatives in Illinois every two or three years; and I think the last time they came was in 1856, when they visited my family at Vermont, Fulton county. Mrs. Chuchwell was one of the kindest, best women I have ever known. She became very much attached to our oldest boy, Frank, who was then about half grown. She wanted Frank to promise her that when he was grown that he would go to Tennessee and visit his old Aunt Moody. She promised him that she would have the negroes dance for him, as she did when his father and uncles visited her, and would make him have a grand and good time.

Well, as time rolled away the boy did go and visit his old aunt, but he did not go in just the way she expected him to come, and he took more company with him than his old aunt was in the habit of entertaining, and he did not wait until he was grown, as his aunt had told him to do.

When the civil war came on and an appeal was made for volunteers, the boy caught the war fever and had it very badly. Because he was so young we did all in our power to persuade him from becoming a soldier; but at last his parents gave their consent and he was enrolled as a member of the old 84th regiment Illinois volunteers, which was made up from men from Fulton and McDonough counties under Col. Waters of Macomb. The regiment was at once ordered to go to east Tennessee, and singular as it may seem took up their headquarters right on Col. Churchwell's fine farm. They certainly could not have found a better locality for a military post if they had searched the state over, for the place was well watered with springs and creeks, with plenty of timber, and with an abundance of houses, barns and stables, and everything that a regiment of men could desire for their comfort and convenience. Col. Waters took possession of their fine old mansion for headquarters of himself and staff, though he was generous enough to let Mrs. Churchwell retain a few of the rooms. Col. Churchwell had died about the commencement of the war, and his only son, William, was an officer in the confederate army, and was killed before the war closed. Mrs. C., with her nephew as overseer, and her negroes, were running her farm when the regiment came down upon them like a cloud of Kansas locusts would upon a fertile field, and with almost as great destruction. It was a terrible ordeal for the old lady to see her beautiful place desecrated, her fine house occupied by soldiers and the soldiers' tents spread over the fields, and her fine carriage horses taken for cavalry horses, and her large Norman horses, which her negroes needed so badly to work the farm, taken to haul some old cannon around over the country; and when she would remonstrate against such treatment the officers would tell her that it was a military necessity. And when her corn and hay would be taken from her barns, and her rails burned, and her dairy and chicken house looted, and her cows milked by the "Yankee bluecoats," then she would lay her grievances before Col. Waters, and he would try to appease her wrath and indignation by telling her that it was a military necessity. These indignities caused her at last to express her mind quite freely as to what she thought of them; so they gave her the name of "old rebel," for she was very bitter against the whole union army.

One day the old lady asked Col. Waters where those fellows came from that had settled down upon her premises, and he told her they were from Illinois. She then told him she had relatives in Illinois by the names of Kirkpatrick and Ross, and wanted to know of the colonel if he had any soldiers by either name. The colonel told her there was a young lad in the regiment whose name was Frank Ross. She said she would like to see him; so the colonel sent one of his officers to hunt Frank up, and after a considerable search he was found in one of the camps frying chickens. He was told there was an old rebel woman up at headquarters who wanted to see him. Frank knew nothing about whose farm it was they were camping on; so he went to the house without any idea as to whom he would meet. But when he came face to face with the "old rebel woman," lo and behold, it was his old Aunt Moody Churchwell—the good old aunt that had invited him to come and visit her, and had promised that when he came she would have the negroes dance and sing for him! But here he was, with a lot of companions, desecrating and wrecking her fine farm and frying her chickens!

But when she saw that he was really Frank, the kind and noble impulses of her heart came to her as in times past, and she showed him the utmost kindness, and told Col. Waters that if the boy should be wounded or get sick to send him to her house and that she would see that he was well taken care of.

Now I must go back and give a sketch of our visit at Col. Churchwell's, where we remained two weeks, visiting him and my wife's relatives in Tennessee. Before starting home the colonel wanted us to have a good time, so he gave us two grand diversions. The first was a negro corn-shucking and the other was a negro dance, or, as they called it, a "negro shindig." If any Northern man ever traveled in the South in slave days and missed a negro corn-shucking or a negro dance, he missed a good deal. The pile of corn was forty feet long, eight feet wide and four or five feet high. They divided it off into two piles and drove a stake in the middle, then chose sides and went at it with a rush. The side that came out last in shucking its pile had to furnish the egg-nogg to treat the whole company. As soon as the negroes commenced shucking the corn, working like beavers, they also commenced singing their plantation songs, and they sang with so much force and power that they could be heard about a mile. While the negroes were thus engaged their wives were preparing for them a bountiful supper. I do not think I ever saw a happier set of people than they were. The colonel had on his negro quarters one house with a large room in it that he said his negroes used to hold meetings in on Sundays, when some white or black preacher would come out from Knoxville and preach for them, and they used the same room to hold their dances in. His rule was to let them have a dance the last Saturday night in each month. He said it encouraged them and made them better servants. So one evening before we came away he gathered the negroes together, men, women, boys and girls, to show us how they could dance. He had one old negro, Ned, who played the violin for them. He told us that he was seventy years old, and had played on "de fiddle" since he was a boy, and seemed to be very proud of his skill. The music and the dancing were both grand, and we looked on with a great deal of delight.

But the time had come for our departure homeward. I had sold the horses and carriage that we had taken with us, and we rode home some of the horses I bought of Col. Churchwell. We bought fourteen head—horses, mares, jacks and jennies. We traveled the first day thirty miles and stopped over night at Arthur Kirkpatrick's, a brother of my wife's father. He was keeping a country store and running a farm. He had some negroes hired to work on the farm, but told us that he would never buy or sell a slave. He had known Gen. Jackson for several years and told us many stories about him; in fact, we could hardly meet an old settler in that state but who could tell us more or less about him.

We came home a different route from the one we went out on. It was nearer, but not so good a road. We came back through Kentucky and through the grand prairies of eastern Illinois. Sometimes we found it twenty miles between the houses. We struck the road we had gone out on at Springfield.

On our way home we passed Major Newton Walker and Hugh Lamaster, who had been to Kentucky and bought a herd of Durham cattle. I think they were the first blooded cattle ever brought into Fulton county. When we reached home I found my wife and little boy, Ossian, anxiously awaiting our arrival, for we had been gone six weeks, and it was a time of joy and rejoicing when we got home, for I had never been away from home before to exceed a day since he was born. And when I opened my satchel and took out the six large apples that Gen. Jackson had given me to take home to my wife and boy (as mentioned in my second letter), our little boy hardly knew whether they were to eat or play with, for he had never seen an apple before. At that time there was not a bearing orchard in Mason county. A few orchards had been planted out, but none of them had commenced to bear. But he soon found that they were good to eat, and his little teeth went for them with a vengeance. I told him that the apples came from Gen. Jackson's orchard—that Jackson had sent them to Ossian and his mother. He had just commenced to learn to talk, and he learned to pronounce the words "Jackson" and "apples" a little before any other words, and after the apples were gone he would often climb up in my lap and put his little arms around my neck and say, "Papa, go to Jackson and get more apples for Ossian." But the apples that came from the orchard of the old hero were the first and the last that he ever had the opportunity to put his little teeth into, for in six weeks after my return he was taken from us by that cruel disease, the croup. He was eighteen months old when he died. He was unusually smart and bright for one of his age, and his death was a terrible bereavement to us, for our very hearts and lives were wrapped up in our little boy. He was our first child, and no tongue could express the grief and sorrow that filled our hearts when he was taken away. Another incident about the child: On the first visit of Col. Churchwell and wife to us in 1842, the little fellow was about six months old. Mrs. Churchwell had a bright, new half-dollar bearing the date "1842." So she got a hole drilled through the rim of it, put a ribbon through it, and hung it around little Ossian's neck, saying it would be a keepsake from her and would show the year the boy was born and the year of their first visit to us. After the lad died his mother laid the coin away, intending to keep it as a sacred memorial as long as she lived, and did keep it for almost forty years. But it was stolen by a servant. His mother would have rather lost a $20 gold piece than that sacred coin.

After we got back from our trip I called on Father Kirkpatrick to give him a few tales of our trip and to tell him about his brothers and sisters, and the great number of nephews and nieces we had met out there, and how anxious they were for him and his wife to go out and make them a visit, and of the kind invitation Gen. Jackson had sent, that if he came to Tennessee again to come and see him. This produced a desire in the old gentleman's heart that he would like to go back to his native state where he had spent his boyhood. So a year after he secured a fine, large horse and carriage and he and his wife made the trip from Canton, Ill., to Knoxville, Tenn., and back without any mishap or accident. He went by the Hermitage, but learned before he got there that the old General had died a few weeks before. But he stopped at the grave with reverence for the old hero with whom he had fought many battles against the Indians; and we may be sure that he paid to his friend and leader the tribute of his tears.

CHAPTER III.

CIRCUMSTANCES SURROUNDING ANDREW JACKSON'S MARRIAGE.—MY VISIT TO THE NOTED BATTLE GROUNDS AT NEW ORLEANS.—STORY OF JACKSON'S GREAT VICTORY.—SOME HIGH OFFICES TO WHICH HE HAD BEEN APPOINTED. A BRIEF REVIEW OF HIS CHILDHOOD.

Now comes the story of how it happened that Jackson was married twice to the same lady. I will give the circumstances surrounding this remarkable case, as I learned them from the people of Tennessee when I was there in 1843, and from his biographies. It was the one event in his long, noble and useful life that gave his enemies a chance to blast his good name and that of his pure and lovely wife These slanders stirred the tiger in him until nothing but human blood would quench his hate. They were the cause of most of his many encounters and duels. It is said that for thirty years he kept his pistols ready for instant use in defense of his wife's good name.

Jackson's wife was a daughter of John Donelson, an old Virginia farmer, who settled five miles from Nashville in 1780, eight years before Jackson came to Tennessee.

Donelson had a family of sons and daughters, and was a man of considerable wealth. He was engaged in raising stock and horses. But one year there came a great drouth that destroyed crops and pastures, and he was compelled to move his family and stock to Mercer county, Ky., 200 miles away, where the drouth had been less severe. While here his daughter Rachel (afterwards Mrs. Jackson) was married to Lewis Robards, who lived with his widowed mother, who at that time was keeping a boarding house; and he took his bride to live with his mother. Boarding with her were some young men, and it was not long until Robards, being of a jealous disposition, and his bride being very handsome, sprightly and jovial, became very jealous of one of the young men and behaved in such an ungentlemanly manner that her indignation was aroused and she wrote to one of her brothers at Nashville to come and take her home—her father and family having returned there. And so she left Robards; but she had only been at home a few weeks when her father, while out surveying, was killed by the Indians. But Mrs. Robards continued to live with her mother, and in about six months her husband relented and made many apologies for his conduct and begged her to come back and live with him. This she consented to do on his promise that he would thereafter treat her with the confidence and respect due a wife; but she refused to return to Kentucky, as it was sparsely settled and the Indians were very troublesome. So instead of her going to Kentucky he came to live with her at Nashville at her mother's house. While they were all living together Gen. Jackson made his first appearance at Nashville. Mrs. Donelson occupied one of the largest houses in the place and was keeping boarders, and it so happened that Jackson became one of her boarders with another young lawyer from South Carolina. And here Gen. Jackson first met the charming bride who was to figure so prominently thereafter in his own life. They could not very well help getting acquainted while they were living in the same house and eating at the same table. It was not long until the green-eyed monster again seized

Robards, and this time it was Gen. Jackson who he thought was paying too much attention to his wife. The result was very scandalous actions on the part of Robards. It grieved the wife terribly, and Gen. Jackson seriously remonstrated with Robards against his cruel and unjust conduct towards his wife and himself, and Jackson at once sought another boarding house. In great indignation the wife again left her husband and took up her abode with a married sister. Robards soon returned to his former home in Kentucky, and commenced proceedings to secure a divorce. The procedure in such cases at that time will interest the reader. I copy from one of Jackson's biographies some of the details:

"In Virginia in the olden time if a man convinced of his wife's infidelity desired to be divorced from her he was required to procure from the legislature an act authorizing an investigation of the charge before a jury and pronouncing the marriage bond dissolved, providing the jury shall find her guilty. In the winter of 1790-91 Lewis Robards of Kentucky, originally part of Virginia, the husband of Rachel Donelson, appeared before the leislature of Virginia with a declaration to the effect that his wife Rachel had deserted him and had lived and was living in adultery with another man, to wit, Andrew Jackson, an attorney at law, whereupon the legislature of Virginia passed an act entitled ' An act concerning the marriage of Lewis Robards,' of which the following is a copy:

"'Be it enacted by the general assembly that it shall and may be lawful for Lewis Robards to sue out of the office of the supreme court of the district of Kentucky a writ against Rachel Robards, which writ shall be framed by the clerk and express the nature of the case, and shall be published for eight weeks in the Kentucky Gazette, whereupon the plaintiff may file his declaration in the same cause, and the defendant may appear and plead to issue, in which case, or if she does not appear within two months after such publication, it shall be set for trial by the clerk on some day in the succeeding court, but may for good cause shown to the court be continued until the succeeding term.'"

Now after the legislature had passed this act Lewis Robards did go on with a suit against his wife for a divorce, and the charge alleged was of desertion and the living in adultery with Andrew Jackson. The legal notice was given in the Gazette, and Mrs. Robards had read it, but she did not attend court or make any defense as she wished him to get the divorce so she could get rid of him. She could have proven by scores of witnesses in Nashville that his allegations were false, for all this time she was living with her mother or sister, while Jackson was living at a hotel.

Some months after this a company of Nashville people was made up to take a trip down the river to Natchez. Among these were Col. Stark and wife, friends of the Donelson family, and Mrs. Robards was asked to go with them, and she did so to visit some friends she had in Natchez. While there she heard the news that Robards had secured a divorce from her. As soon as Jackson heard the news he took a steamboat for Natchez and married Mrs. Robards and took her back to Nashville. The marriage was on a license and in due form of law. After they had lived happily together for six months the astonishing word came to them that the divorce had just been granted, that the first report was a mistake. It was really about two years after Robards had commenced divorce proceedings before the divorce was granted. At that time there were no mails being carried between Hardin county, Kentucky, and Nashville, and it was difficult to get news from one section to another. Gen. and Mrs. Jackson were greatly shocked when this news came to them. There was but one thing to do. All their friends agreed to that. They must procure another license and be married the second time according to the due forms of law. This was done at once. It did not affect their high social position in Nashville, for all the people knew they had done no intentional wrong. Thereafter inside of six years Gen. Jackson was elected one of the trustees of the Davidson

University with the most eminent ministers and other citizens as his colleagues; then as a member of Tennessee's first constitutional convention; then to the lower house of Congress; then to the United States Senate, and finally to be a judge of the Supreme Court of Tennessee. All these high honors and responsibilities came to him within six years after his marriage to Mrs. Robards, and without protest or criticism as to that act.

It was not until the opening of the vile presidential campaign of 1828 that politicians and the newspapers opened the vials of scandal and detraction upon the old hero and his pure and noble wife. The old records were searched and the worst possible construction put upon every act. As I have said in a former article, there were no great national issues in that campaign, but the men were voted for on their records, and this vile abuse was resorted to defeat the old hero of many wars.

I will now tell of my visit to the battle-ground of New Orleans, where Gen. Jackson defeated Major Edward Packingham on the 8th of January, 1815, and will describe its appearance, and give some of the circumstances of the battle as I gleaned them from citizens who lived there in New Orleans at the time.

It was in the fall of 1856 that, with my wife and little boy Joseph, I took a trip by river to New Orleans, and thence by the gulf to Texas. We took a steamer at Browning on the Illinois river to St. Louis, and there took another steamer for the long river trip down the Mississippi to New Orleans. We stopped there a week, and put up at the Planters' Hotel. I found that the landlord was an old hotel keeper and well acquainted with the older residents of that country, and he found for me a man that was in the city when the battle was fought, to go with me and show me the battlefield, and explain the circumstances connected with it. The battlefield was then about five miles from the city, and hacks were running there every day at fifty cents for the trip. So under this guide we had a good view of the whole situation. A ditch had been dug and breastworks thrown up from the Mississippi river a distance of a mile to a low, swampy land. At the time of the battle the ditch contained five feet of water, and the breastworks were from five to six feet high, made from the dirt that was taken out of the ditch. There was also many cotton bales used in building the fortification. When I was there the greater part of the breastworks had been leveled off and the ditch filled up; but still there was enough left to show its location and how it had been constructed. It appeared that Gen. Jackson had used a great deal of skill and ingenuity in constructing the fortifications to shield his men from the fire of their enemies. On the back side of the breastworks a platform of earth had been constructed a foot high and five feet wide, upon which the men could step to fire over the works and then step down out of range of the enemies' bullets to reload their guns.

From the best information I could get from old citizens and other sources, I have no doubt that in this battle the British forces numbered about 7,000 men, while Jackson's army numbered 5,000. Gen. Jackson had declared martial law at New Orleans because of the many enemies in the city, and he had conscripted some thousand Frenchmen, Creoles, etc., that knew very little about military matters.

One singular thing happened at this battle that is worth recording. Packingham had caused to be constructed a supply of ladders and plank platforms to be used in crossing the ditch and climbing the earthworks to Jackson's stronghold; but when the battle commenced and Packingham made his assault and came to the ditch, they had forgotten to bring along those platforms and ladders. So the only way they had of crossing the ditch was for one man to take another on his shoulders and wade through the water that was five feet deep. While they were crossing the ditch in this absurd manner hundreds of them were shot down, and the forces repulsed. A second assault was then made, but with no better success. Then Gen. Packingham made a third attempt to rally his men, leading them himself; but as he came near the ditch he was shot off his horse, one ball going through his arm and another piercing his thigh, and his horse was killed under him. The British army found it impossible to endure such a fire, that had slaughtered them by hundreds at a time, so they gave up the fight and fled. It was found after the battle that over 2,000 British soldiers lay prostrate on the battlefield—500 dead and 1,500 wounded. Jackson's loss was six men killed and seven wounded. It was the greatest victory ever achieved in the United States, when we take into consideration the fact the battle was fought in less than an hour.

I can remember away back in the year 1828, when Gen. Jackson ran for president, that one of the means resorted to to thrill and inspire the hearts of the people was the war songs. At that time they had no brass bands or French horns. The only martial music was the fife and drum, supplemented with patriotic songs. One of these was called "The Battle of New Orleans." It described the parts that the Kentucky and Tennessee boys had taken in the battle, and when sung by a dozen or more strong voices it had a most animating effect on the old soldiers and the crowds of people that would gather to listen to them.

When I was on the battlefield I was anxious to get some relics to carry home with me. While trying to get a spade to hunt for bullets, etc., I was told that the ground had been dug over so often that I would find nothing. But I met a Dutchman who had many relics of the battle. He had three bullets which he called the "Packingham Balls," which he claimed to have found near the spot where Gen. Packingham was slain. One was a rifle ball, one a large musket ball and the other a grape shot about the size of a black walnut. His supposition was that the rifle ball was the one that had gone through Packingham's arm, that the musket ball was the one that had gone through his thigh and that the large ball had killed his horse. I believed that he was an honest Dutchman and did find the balls on the battlefield, though I did not take much stock in the tale about the balls killing Packingham, although it might have happened. But I thought it would be a good story to tell when I got home, so I paid $2 for the balls.

After remaining a week at New Orleans we took boat

over the gulf for Galveston, Texas, where we remained for a few days, and then went down to Port Lavaca, where I bought a span of ponies and a light carriage, and spent the winter traveling over the country. If a storm, or what is called in Texas a "norther," came up, we would stop a few days at some town or farm house until it was over. It so happened that when we got to Austin, the capital of the state, on the 8th of January, we found the people were holding a grand demonstration in honor of Jackson and the victory of New Orleans. I learned that the 8th of January was celebrated as a regular holiday in most of the towns and cities in the state.

Here in California the 8th of January has been observed as a public holiday since the state was settled. Here in the City of Oakland we had one of the grandest celebrations January 8th, 1897, that has ever taken place in the city, in honor of Gen. Jackson and his great victory. It was the occasion of the dedication of a fine school house that we had just completed at a cost of $200,000. We were not able to procure a hickory pole large enough to bear the national flag, as hickory timber does not grow wild here as it does in Illinois. But it happened that a family came out from Illinois several years ago and brought with them some hickory nuts, one of which was planted in her father's door yard by a little daughter, and it grew to be a fine tree. On the day of the dedication the young lady presented this tree to the school board, and they planted it on the school grounds in honor of "Old Hickory."

Many eloquent speeches were made on this occasion, but one of the speakers, after a grand eulogy of Gen. Jackson, declared that after he was elected president he turned every whig out of office and put a democrat in his place, and that no whig could hold an office under his administration. It was a great mistake. I remember that my father, who was a strong whig, and did all he could for the election of Adams, soon after the election of 1828 moved to Havana, Illinois, when Jackson appointed him postmaster at that place. He also appointed Abraham Lincoln, another ardent whig, to be postmaster at New Salem, in the place of

Samuel Hill, who was a democrat. I knew of many other cases in which Gen. Jackson had appointed whigs to office. The great question with him was, "Is he honest, and is he capable?" which had more to do with his appointments than the question of politics.

The many high and important offices that Gen. Jackson was elected to and appointed to, and some of them at a time when he was quite a young man, will show the confidence and the high regard in which he was held, not only by his own state, but by the whole nation, for he was elected State's Attorney, Judge of the Circuit Court, and also Judge of the Supreme Court of Tennessee, a member of Congress and a United States Senator, all before he was thirty-one years of age. In 1824 he ran for president, his opponents being John Quincy Adams, W. H. Crawford and Henry Clay, and out of 261 electoral votes cast he got 99, Adams 84, Crawford 47 and Clay 37, and in the popular vote he got a majority over Adams of 50,551 votes. Neither of the candidates having received a majority of all the votes, it was carried into the House, and by some maneuvering Adams was counted in and Jackson counted out. In 1828 he ran again for president against John Quincy Adams, receiving 178 of the electoral votes to Adams 83, and a majority over Adams of the popular vote of 158,134. He ran again in 1832 against Henry Clay, Jackson receiving 218 of the electoral votes and Clay 49, and a majority of the popular vote of 157,313.

I must close these sketches of Gen. Jackson with a brief review of his childhood. I have taken great pains to get these interesting facts in a reliable form.

Gen. Jackson's parents were Scotch-Irish, coming from the north of Ireland. His father's name was Andrew Jackson; his mother's, Elizabeth Hutchinson. When they came to America they had two sons, Hugh and Robert. Mrs. J. had three sisters who came with them to America. They settled in the Waxhaw settlement on Waxhaw creek, named for an Indian tribe that occupied that country. It is now Union county, North Carolina. They settled on a farm as a renter (this was in 1765), and within two years the father died. The mother then moved in with her brother-in-law, George McCamis, and in a week after the father's death Andrew was born, March 15, 1767. In two months she went with her children to live with another brother-in-law, Thomas Crawford, who had married another sister of hers. This sister was an invalid, and Mrs. Jackson took charge of the family and lived there most of the time until her death fifteen years later. Her son Hugh worked for his uncle, McCamis, until the breaking out of the Revolutionary war, when he enlisted as a patriot and soon died of the hardships and privations of army life. Her remaining sons, Robert and Andrew, were not old enough to go into the army, but were called into the service, with many other boys of the settlement, to guard and protect their homes and property against the British soldiers who were making raids upon them, destroying property, stealing horses, etc. All the older men had gone to war, leaving the women and boys to stand guard about their homes. While Robert and Andrew and other boys were thus engaged a company of red-coats came upon them and took them prisoners and marched them off to Camden, a British garrison forty miles away. After they had been prisoners a few weeks, Mrs. Jackson, who was a brave and resolute woman, determined that she would go to Camden and try to get her sons released. So she set out for the British garrison on horseback and alone. When she got to the fort she found her two boys in a terrible predicament. They had had an encounter with one of the British officers and had been cruelly treated. The officer had ordered Andrew to clean and black his boots, which he refused to do, telling the officer that although he was a prisoner of war, he would not black his boots. The officer struck him on the head with his sword, when Andrew threw up his hands to guard off the blow he received a cut on his arm, and also on the side of his head, the scars of which he carried to his grave. The officer then ordered Robert to clean and black his boots; he also refused to do it, and the officer knocked him down and beat him terribly.

So when Mrs. Jackson found her boys in prison, she found that in addition to their wounds that both had taken the small-pox, which was raging at a terrible rate in the prison. She went to the chief officer and plead for their deliverance, and succeeded in getting them released. She then procured another horse, and they started home on their forty-mile ride. When they got within an hour's ride of their home there came up a dreadful rain that drenched them to the skin. It very greatly aggravated the small-pox, and Robert died a few days after she had gotten him home. Andrew barely escaped death by the kind and careful nursing of his mother.

Two months after word came to the settlement from Charleston, S. C., which was then in possession of the British army, that great distress and suffering and sickness were prevailing among the American prisoners there. A number of the prisoners were from the Waxhaw settlement, and among them were several of her nephews. Mrs. Jackson was prevailed upon to go with two other ladies to Charleston with clothing, medicines, etc., for the prisoners, and also to secure, if possible, their release or exchange. So she started with her two friends on the long journey of 150 miles, on horseback; and when they got there they found that the prisoners were confined on a ship, and that the ship fever was prevailing among them. So after ministering to the wants of the soldiers and doing what they could for their relief, they started on their journey home. They stopped one night at a farm house, when Mrs. Jackson was taken down with the ship fever contracted while on the ship, and growing worse, died in a few days, and was buried in that locality. It was sad news to take back to Andrew and their friends. Nothing could be done about bringing back her remains, because it was a long distance, and the weather was hot, and besides that they were poor people. Andrew, at the time of her death, was fifteen years old, and his father, mother, brothers and sisters were all dead. But he continued to live with his uncle, Thomas Crawford, and attended the school in the log school house. The branches taught were reading, writing, geography and arithmetic.

His mother had often spoken of her wish to educate him for a Presbyterian minister, and would have tried to do so if she had lived. He often spoke of his good, Christian mother, and with much sorrow of her sad death and burial, for she sacrificed her life for others.

When Gen. Jackson was a member of Congress the first time he employed two men to go and see if they could find his mother's grave, and if so, to remove her body to the place where his father was buried. But the men could not find her grave. There was no stone to mark the spot, and the country had undergone many changes, so that there was no clue to her burial place. It was all the loving and loyal son could do.

When he was a candidate for the presidency in 1828, and every vile thing that could be hatched up was told about him, it was said that his wife came into his room one day when he was reading a newspaper, and found him in tears. On her inquiry about what the trouble was, he showed her a paragraph in the newspaper stating that his mother had been a washer-woman and filled a pauper's grave. He said to his wife:

"I can defend your character and mine; but when they assail my devoted mother, it almost breaks my heart."

There was one grand and noble trait of character in the General that drew people to him with hooks of steel. I was told by men who had been with him in the army how kind and considerate he was to his soldiers. In one of their long marches from Natchez to Nashville, a distance of 500 miles through a wilderness country, the officers, of course, were on horseback, while the soldiers were afoot. Often the General would fall back to the rear to look after the sick and disabled soldiers, and it was common for him to dismount and place some sick or lame soldier on his horse, while he trudged along on foot with the men day after day through the miry road, gay and cheerful, inspiring his men with his splendid courage and unselfishness. It was on this long and dreadful march that he got the name of "Hickory." In the first place one of the soldiers remarked: "The general is tough." Then another said: "He is as tough as hickory." Then they commenced to call him "Hickory Jackson," and as he advanced in age, they applied to him the name "Old Hickory," and the honored name followed him to his death.

In tracing the life of Gen. Jackson we find many things to admire. In the first place he was born into the world with a good, strong constitution, with good common-sense, and with a good back-bone, so that he was always ready to stand up for the rights of the people. But the great and crowning glory of his life was his grand and glorious victory at New Orleans with his Kentucky and Tennessee militia, over the renowned Major-General Sir Edward Packingham of the British army with his chosen and well-drilled soldiers. No doubt the General, in looking over that battlefield, strewn with the bodies of 2,000 enemies slain and wounded, while his loss was but five killed and seven wounded, must have felt something of exultation over the foe that had so cruelly treated him and his brothers and caused the death of his beloved mother.

General Jackson's parents were Scotch-Irish Presbyterians, and he inherited their reverence for religion and for ministers. He was always a generous contributor to the church and religious institutions. Previous to his wife's death he gave her a solemn promise that he would unite with the church and live a Christian's life. This promise he complied with about five years before his death. He united with the Presbyterian church, and was asked to accept the office of ruling elder, but declined the office. He said:

"I am too young in the church for such an office. My countrymen," he said, "have given me high honors, but I should esteem the office of ruling elder in the church of Jesus Christ a far higher honor than any I have ever received."

He was strongly attached to his slaves, and in his will he distributed them among his wife's relatives, so that they should not be sold outside the family. But the time came for him to die. His faculties were clear and bright up to the hour of his death. He called his family and servants about his bed and said he wanted to meet them all in Heaven, black and white. He said he was ready and prepared to go, that death was only the dark pathway opening into a blessed and endless life. The funeral sermon was preached by Rev. Dr. Edgar, of Nashville, from the text, "These are they which came out of great tribulation and washed their robes white in the blood of the Lamb." It was the largest funeral ever known in Nashville, except that of his beloved wife.

This country has had few men honored and beloved by the masses of the people as was Gen. Jackson. For many long years will his noble deeds and sacrifices and his sacred memory be cherished deep down in the hearts of a grateful country and a generous people.

Peter Cartwright.

CHAPTER I.

MR. CARTWRIGHT'S SUCCESSFUL EFFORTS TO DEFEAT SLAVERY.—HIS REMOVAL TO ILLINOIS IN 1824.

When Peter Cartwright came from Kentucky to Sangamon county in 1823 and bought a farm seven miles west of Springfield, he found the people greatly agitated (as I have said in a former letter) over the question whether Illinois should be a slave or free state. An election to settle the question was called for the first Monday in August, 1824. He had left Kentucky to get away from slavery, and it was natural, with his combative disposition, that he should go into the battle for freedom with all his soul and might. He thoroughly canvassed the counties of Sangamon and Morgan, making speeches against slavery in all the churches and schoolhouses, or wherever he could get an audience.

At that time there were but thirty counties in the state, and Sangamon and Morgan were the two northern counties on the east side of the Illinois river. Pike and Fulton were the only counties on the west side of the river. Fulton was the extreme northern county, taking in Fort Clark (now Peoria) and Galena and Chicago.

There was at that time in Fulton county a man who perhaps did as much to defeat slavery as did Mr. Cartwright or any other man in Illinois. His name was Ossian M. Ross. He thoroughly canvassed the counties of Fulton and Pike. He was a Quaker, and the Quakers were bitterly opposed to human slavery. He went into the conflict with all his might, and never ceased until the votes were counted and the battle of freedom won. I believe there was more credit due him and Peter Cartwright for carrying the state against slavery than any other two men in Illinois. Following is the vote on that question. The vote of Morgan, Sangamon, Pike and Fulton will show how well they succeeded.

THE VOTE ON SLAVERY.

	For.	Against.
Alexander	75	51
Bond	63	240
Clark	32	116
Crawford	134	262
Edgar	3	234
Edwards	186	371
Fayette	125	121
Franklin	170	113
Fulton	5	60
Gallatin	596	133
Greene	134	405
Hamilton	173	86
Jackson	180	93
Jefferson	90	43
Johnson	74	74
Lawrence	158	261
Madison	351	58
Marion	45	53
Montgomery	74	99
Monroe	171	196
Morgan	43	555
Pike	23	261
Pope	275	124
Randolph	357	184
Sangamon	153	722
St. Clair	427	543
Union	213	240
Washington	112	173
Wayne	189	111
White	355	326
Total	4950	6822

Majority against slavery..................1872

After Mr. Cartwright had finished his fight against slavery he returned to Kentucky to finish his preparations for removal to Illinois. In the fall of 1824 he started with two wagons drawn by horses for his new home in the wilderness of Illinois. They met with some sad misfortunes on the road. At one time one of the wagons was overturned, seriously injuring one of his daughters. While encamped one night in the great forest a tree fell upon another daughter, crushing her to death. They had to carry the mangled body twenty miles before they could procure a coffin and give the child decent burial.

When they arrived at their new home Mr. Cartwright found that the election had gone to his satisfaction. Notwithstanding slavery had been voted down by the decisive majority of 1,872 votes, the slavery party was not annihilated. They pretended to believe that their vote had not all turned out, and hoped that they might win in another election. They had a large majority in both branches of the legislature, and were determined to secure another election. It was true that Edward Coles, an anti-slavery man, had been elected governor; but there had been four candidates, and the slavery vote had been divided, causing Coles to be elected by a small majority.

In the early settlement of Illinois the southern part of the state was settled first, and mainly by people from the slave states. These people brought with them their slave laws, slave prejudices, and many of them also brought their slaves. They found that many of the staple products of the South, such as hemp, tobacco and cotton, could be raised in southern Illinois, and they believed that these products could not be profitably raised without slave labor. There was another condition that influenced the people to favor slavery: About that time a tremendous emigration was pouring through southern Illinois into Missouri from Virginia and Kentucky. In the fall of the year every great road was crowded with these movers in long trains of teams, and with their negroes, and with plenty of money. They were the wealthiest and best educated emigrants from the slave states. The early settlers of Illinois saw it all and with great envy for Missouri's good fortune. The lordly emigrant as he passed along with his droves of negroes and piles of money took malicious delight in adding to the unrest by pretending to regret the short-sighted policy of Illinois which excluded him by declaring against the institution of slavery. This gave the people of southern Illinois a strong desire to hold another election, hoping that slavery might be voted in.

And so the agitation was kept up from year to year. The same infamous old "black laws" were still on the statute book, and many negroes were held in slavery, especially in the southern counties along the Ohio and Mississippi rivers. They were hemmed in by slave states, Kentucky on the southeast and Missouri on the west. So the sentiment was strong for slavery. There were but few men in the legislature who dared oppose these bad laws or slavery. It would have been a very unpopular if not dangerous step. Then there was great fear of being called an "abolitionist," the most odious epithet that in those times could be applied to a man.

But in 1828 there was to be an election for representatives, and the friends of free territory prevailed upon Mr. Cartwright to become a candidate, and he was elected without much opposition from the northern counties. He believed that he could for a few months serve his God and his country as acceptably in the general assembly as in preaching the gospel.

By this time the northern counties were settling up with people from the East, and the tide turned forever against the friends of slavery. Mr. Cartwright with the help of other members of the legislature was able to have some of the infamous "black laws" repealed and excellent laws enacted in their stead. It was a grand and noble work. I may have more to say on this subject in a later sketch.

CHAPTER II.

MR. CARTWRIGHT AS A GREAT PREACHER AND A GREAT ORGANIZER.—THE JACKSONVILE ORDINANCE AND HOW MR. CARTWRIGHT ASSISTED IN ITS ENFORCEMENT.

When Peter Cartwright came to Illinois in 1824, and settled seven miles east of Springfield, at what was afterwards known as Pleasant Plains, he found the country very sparsely settled. Sangamon county at that time extended north as far as the northern part of the state, the settlements were few and far between and there was not a church within the boundaries of the county. Springfield was a small village, and the only place they had for public worship was a small frame school house, but in about a year after Mr. Cartwright came to that place the Methodist and Presbyterian congregations joined in building a small brick church, which was the first brick building erected in Springfield. The two congregations used this building alternately for two years, when the Methodists sold out their interest in the property and built for themselves a frame church much larger in size.

Mr. Cartwright possessed too much of a missionary spirit, however, to settle down in one place. He looked upon the whole state of Illinois as his field of labor, and would travel from place to place, organizing a church and Sunday school wherever he could find a few families gathered together, and preaching in the homes of the people and in log school houses. But his great forte in carrying on his missionary and evangelical work was his campmeetings. He would hold ten-day campmeetings in every part of the country, and people would flock from miles around to attend them.

Mr. Cartwright was not only a great preacher, but it might be said of him, as of Lincoln, that he was a born leader. He was a great organizer, and had held the office of presiding elder ever since he was twenty-two years old.

He had a most excellent control over his members, and would allow no drones in his camp. In those primitive times it was not considered necessary that a teacher of religion should be a scholar. It was thought to be his business to preach from a knowledge of the Scriptures and the guiding and controlling influence of the Holy Spirit. Their wonderful success at those meetings might be attributed to the earnestness and zeal with which they pictured the blessings of Heaven and the awful torments of the wicked in fire and brimstone. They believed with certainty that they saw the souls of wicked men rushing headlong to perdition, and they stepped forward to warn and to save with all the self-devotion of a generous man who risks his own life to save that of a drowning neighbor. And to these earnest, Christian people are we indebted for the spread of the protestant religion through Illinois at that early day. At many of those campmeetings there would be from 200 to 300 conversions.

In 1832 the democratic party again brought out Peter Cartwright for the legislature. He was a farmer as well as a preacher, and was very popular with the farmers. He had also given good satisfaction in the legislature, to which he was elected in 1828, having been instrumental in repealing several of the obnoxious laws which had disgraced the state, and the people wanted to send him back. This time he defeated Abraham Lincoln. When he was in the legislature he had two prohibition laws enacted. One was that no saloon or drinking house should be permitted within one mile of Jacksonville, and was known as the "Jacksonville Ordinance." The Jacksonville college had been established, and was then the only college in the state. The other prohibitive law was that no saloon or drinking house should be erected or permitted to run within one mile of a campmeeting. Mr. Cartwright had an opportunity to assist in enacting this latter law in Fulton county in 1833. He had erected a campmeeting on the west side of Canton, near where the old Methodist church stood. There was then a handsome grove of timber standing there. They had got their shed and preacher's stand put up and everything in order for the meeting when a man from Canton set up a huckster's stand with cigars, tobacco, and all kinds of ardent spirits within a few rods of the campgrounds. Mr. Cartwright went to him and told him he would have to move his drinking establishment, as it was against the law to sell liquor within a mile of a campmeeting. The man told him he had plenty of friends to back him and he would continue to sell, so Cartwright swore out a warrant for his arrest and had him taken before Esquire Stillman for trial. A young lawyer in Canton defended the prisoner, while Cartwright prosecuted the case. The court imposed a fine of $10, which the huckster said he would not pay, so the necessary papers were made out committing him to the county jail. But the man defied the constable, telling him that he could not find men enough in Canton to take him. The constable was completely cowed, as he was afraid of the man's friends who had promised to protect him, but Mr. Cartwright told the constable to summons him and two of his church members and they would take him. One of the churchmen went into the woods and cut a stout hickory cane for each of the three, and they hoisted the man on a horse and started for Lewistown. He believed that his friends would rescue him from the officers and kept looking back every few miles to see if they were coming, but they never made their appearance, and when they got in sight of Lewistown the man gave up all hope and paid his fine. They all turned back for Canton, but that put a stop to setting up saloons near campmeetings in Fulton county. At the close of this campmeeting Mr. Cartwright reported that ninety persons had been soundly converted and among them were some of the hard cases about Canton.

CHAPTER III.

THE NAME OF PETER CARTWRIGHT FAMILIAR THROUGHOUT THE STATE.—HIS EFFORTS TO DRIVE OUT THE MORMONS.—GRAND OVATION TENDERED HIM IN 1869.—HIS LABORS AT EIGHTY-SIX YEARS OF AGE.—AN INCIDENT OF HIS LAST MISSIONARY TOUR.

The career of Peter Cartwright has been one of the most remarkable and eventful known in the history of the great northwest. There was scarcely a town or village or city in Illinois where the name of Peter Cartwright was not familiar. He had been for sixty-five years an effective itinerant Methodist preacher, not having lost six months' labor in that long period of time. During that period he served as presiding elder fifty years. He had wonderful powers of oratory, and often at his campmeetings there would be 200 to 300 conversions under his preaching.

He first visited that section of country between the Illinois and Mississippi rivers in 1827. He crossed the Illinois river at Beardstown, and traveled across the country to Atlas on the Mississippi river, that town then being the county seat of Pike county. He there found some ten or twelve families, and among them were three brothers, William, John and Leonard Ross. They had laid out the town of Atlas. They came from the state of New York. They had bought up considerable land in that vicinity. Mr. Cartwright stopped with William Ross over night and attended a campmeeting that was held ten miles from Atlas, which was the first campmeeting held in Pike county. The same fall he held a campmeeting in Schuyler county, near Rushville. He came into Fulton county, stayed at my father's house in Lewistown over night, and preached that evening in the log courthouse at Lewistown. He went from there to Canton, where he attended a campmeeting that was held in a beautiful grove of timber on the west side of Canton. That was the second campmeeting that was held in the county. After the campmeeting was over he took a trip up into the Rock river country that was then settled with Indians. His great and sympathetic heart went out for the good and welfare of the poor Indians, as well as for the white people. He believed that civilizing and Christianizing them was far better than fighting them. He was instrumental in having his church establish a mission among the Pottawattomie Indians, which was located on Rock river; and it might truthfully be said that he was the first missionary that labored among those wild Indians. He was appointed superintendent of the mission and conducted it with much ability until the Indians were driven out of the country during the Black Hawk war.

Mr. Cartwright was always in politics a democrat of the Andrew Jackson stamp. He was twice elected a member of the Illinois legislature, his opponent at one time being Abraham Lincoln, who ran on the Whig ticket. That party being in the majority in his district at the time, Mr. Lincoln was elected by a small majority.

Mr. Cartwright was a descendant of a loyal and patriotic ancestry, his father having served for two and one-half years in the War of the Revolution for American Independence; and when the War of the Rebellion in the south took place, and Mr. Lincoln called for volunteers, Mr. Cartwright rushed to Springfield and hoisted the American flag on the top of the Methodist church in that city, and used all of his influence to put down the Rebellion.

Mr. Cartwright, who had labored so heroically when he first came to Illinois to prevent the planting of the institution of slavery on the soil of that state, found, after he had lived in the state about twenty years, that an effort was being made to plant another institution over the state which he regarded as being almost as pernicious and vile as that of slavery, and that was Mormonism, which included polygamy, and his righteous indignation was aroused to the highest pitch. For the Mormons, who had been driven out of Missouri for their bad conduct, had crossed the Mississippi and had spread themselves over several of the counties in Illinois, and their preachers and elders traveled through every town and neighborhood and were very zealous in propagating their doctrines and winning over converts to their religion; and they also took an active part in the politics of the times, and at all elections they cast their votes as a unit; and in some of the counties they had elected some of their elders to seats in the legislature and to fill county offices. So Peter Cartwright got after the Mormons with all the power and might that he possessed, and did much to check their pernicious and mischievous conduct in many localities.

After Mr. Cartwright had been elected the fiftieth time as a presiding elder, his church, which convened in conference at Quincy in 1868, passed a resolution that at their next conference, that was to be held at Lincoln in 1869, that a grand ovation, or a kind of jubilee, should be given him in honor of his fifty years' service as presiding elder. At that conference a very large number of ministers were present—the largest that had ever before assembled in Illinois. Also a number of ministers came from other states to pay their homage and respect to the grand old veteran. Rev. I. P. Newman came all the way from Washington City to see him. Many eloquent speeches were made, many letters of congratulations were read, and many handsome and costly presents were given him. Among the letters read were notable ones from Ex-Governors Richard Yates and R. J. Oglesby. In Governor Yates' letter, among the many good things he had to say about the old elder, was the following:

"During the war, when the governor of the state needed the support of all good men in the union cause, he felt cheered and strengthened by the earnest approval and strong influence of Peter Cartwright."

In Gov. Oglesby's letter he said:

"For as long as I can remember, the name of Peter Cartwright has been a household word in our western country. Bold, honest, earnest and untiring, he has stood on the frontier of advancing civilization to proclaim the truth of God and history. It is the completion of his semi-centennial eldership of your church. A jubilee such as this can come to few men. Few are favored with such length of life in which to do good for mankind."

At the jubilee conference Gov. Oglesby sent to the committee a beautiful and magnificent chair with his compliments, as follows:

"I will thank you to present the chair sent to your care to Elder Cartwright, and request that he will accept it as a testimonial of friendship and respect, upon which, in the weary days of an honorable old age, he may occasionally be seated to rest from his labors.

"R. J. OGLESBY."

At the time of the jubilee conference Elder Cartwright was eighty-four years of age, though he lived to his eighty-seventh year, and his wife lived to the age of eighty-six. They lived together as husband and wife for sixty-four years. They had nine children (two sons and seven daughters), fifty grandchildren, thirty-seven great-grandchildren and one great-great-grandson. Three of their daughters married traveling Methodist Episcopal ministers, two of whom had been presiding elders; and all of their children, and many of their grandchildren and great-grandchildren, were members of the Methodist Episcopal church.

After the jubilee conference was over, in 1869, Mr. Cartwright concluded that he would retire from further labors and spend the balance of his days with his wife on their beautiful farm at Pleasant Plains where they had lived for forty years. The old elder stood it bravely for six months, and then he became restless and uneasy, and his old propensity and desire for preaching and the distribution of religious books and tracts came back upon him so that he could stand leisure and idleness no longer. So he packed a carpet-sack with religious literature and started off on a missionary tour. He traveled through several of the states and territories, and on his return he said the following:

"I will furnish a brief statement of my labors during this year. I have dedicated eight churches, preached at seventy-seven funerals, addressed eight schools, baptized twenty adults and fifty children, married five couples, received fifteen into the church on probation and twenty-five into full connection; have raised $25 missionary money; have donated $20 for new churches, written 112 letters, received in donations $50, and for my lectures and sermons $700; for traveling expenses $650, and sold $200 worth of books."

Now that was certainly a good account of stewardship for a year's labor by a man that was eighty-six years of age.

Mr. Cartwright, on his return from his last year's missionary tour, had many circumstances and incidents of very great interest to relate, and I will relate one of them: He had taken his seat in the cars one day when a lady came and introduced herself to him, stating that he had baptized her when she was a child, and that then she had a large family, who were with her in the cars; that they were moving to a distant part of the country, away from church privileges, and she wanted him to baptize her family. When the conductor came into the car he told him that this lady desired him to baptize her children, and asked him if he would allow him the privilege. The conductor told him that there were a great many passengers on the cars who were in a hurry to get through, and he could not stop the train. He told the conductor that if he would grant him the privilege he could baptize them if his train was running at lightning speed. The conductor told him to go ahead; and when water was brought he baptized the family and sent them on their way rejoicing; and he would gladly have baptized the whole car-load if they had been fit subjects for baptism.

There are few ministers, if any, that have lived in the last century that can show such a record of long and faithful service in the Christian faith; and for many long years will his noble deeds and sacrifices be remembered and his sacred memory be cherished deep down in the hearts of a grateful country and a generous people. It would be right and proper that a monument should be erected to his sacred memory, the same as has been done over the grave of the noble Lincoln.

MY AUTOBIOGRAPHY BRIEFLY SKETCHED.

MY ANCESTORS, THE ROSS AND LEE FAMILIES.—THEIR DESCENDANTS AND SOME OF THEIR DEEDS.—THE JOURNEY OF MY FAMILY FROM NEW YORK TO ILLINOIS.—SOME OF MY EARLY PERSONAL ADVENTURES.—MY MARRIAGE TO JANE R. KIRKPATRICK, JANUARY 1ST, 1840.—MY PERSONAL WORK IN THE EARLY DEVELOPMENT OF THE COUNTRY.—THE OFFICES HELD AND MY WORK AS A DELEGATE TO THE NATIONAL PROHIBITION CONVENTION IN THE YEAR 1884.—THE SIXTY YEARS OF MY MEMBERSHIP IN THE PRESBYTERIAN CHURCH.

In closing my pioneer history of Fulton county, I thought that it would be proper and right for me to give a short biographical sketch of my own life and also of some of my ancestors, as some of my children and grandchildren and great-grandchildren might have the curiosity to know something about their genealogy, and where their ancestors came from, and I will therefore give such genealogy as far as I have been able to trace it back to the Ross and the Lee families.

My great-grandfather, Zebulon Ross, came from Scotland to America, and settled in Dutchess county, New York, in the year 1728, and died in the same county at the age of ninety years. He had a son, Joseph Ross, who was married to Abigail Lee, a daughter of Thomas Lee. Thomas Lee was a soldier in the Revolutionary War, and it was after him that the Lee part of my name was given me, which is Harvey Lee Ross.

My grandmother, Abigail Lee Ross, came to Illinois in 1824, and died at my father's house in Havana, Illinois, in 1834. I have often heard her tell of her father, Thomas Lee, being a soldier in the Revolutionary War. Thomas Lee's ancestors came from England to America about the middle of the seventeenth century. There were two branches of the Lee family, one of which branches settled in the state of New York and the other in the state of Virginia. Both branches came from the same original stock. Their ancestors had held positions of honor and trust in the old country, and some of those who settled in New York and Virginia occupied prominent places in the colonial history of America, in the state legislatures, and in the councils of the nation. Joshua Lee, brother of Thomas Lee, was for many years a member of the New York State Senate. One of the Virginia branch, Richard Henry Lee, drew up and submitted to Congress the resolution of June 7th, 1776, declaring that the United Colonies of America are and ought to be free and independent states; that they absolved themselves from all allegiance to the British Crown, and that all political connection between them and Great Britain is and ought to be totally absolved, which resolution was adopted by the Continental Congress. Both Richard Henry Lee and his brother, Francis Lightfoot Lee, were members of the Continental Congress and signers of the Declaration of Independence.

Thomas Lee, the father of Abigail Lee, was born in Fishkill, New York, November 15th, 1739, and died at Penn Yan, New York, January 22nd, 1814. His wife, Mattie Sherman, was born in 1743, and died October 14th, 1833.

Thomas Lee and Mattie Sherman were married in 1760, and had ten children. Their oldest daughter, Abigail Lee, was born in 1760, and married Joseph Ross.

Joseph Ross and Abigail Lee had born to them the following children: Joseph, Ossian M., Matthias, Thomas L., John N., Eliza, Maria and Sallie.

Ossian M. Ross was born in Dutchess county, New York, August 16th, 1790, and died at Havana, Illinois, in 1837. His wife, Mary Winans, was born in New Jersey, April 1st, 1793, and died at Peoria, Illinois, in 1875. Ossian M. Ross and Mary Winans were married in Seneca county, New York, July 7th, 1811. There was born to them the following children: Lewis W., Harriet M., Harvey Lee, Leonard F., Lucinda C. and Pike C. Ross.

The services of Thomas Lee in assisting in the establishment of American independence during the war of the Revolution were as follows: He was second lieutenant of Captain Jack Rosekrance's company, Col. Jack Holmes, fourth regiment, New York Continental line, 28th of June, 1775; promoted first lieutenant, August 3rd, 1775. He was captain of the eighth company, fifth regiment, New York Continental line, commanded by Col. Louis Du Bois, November 21st, 1776; resigned May 19th, 1778. He was also captain in Col. Zepharriah Platt's regiment of New York Associated Exempts, October 19th, 1779. He was also captain in Col. Louis Du Bois' regiment of New York militia, July 1st, 1780. (References, pages 140, 231, 257, 285 and 529 of Vol. 1, "New York in the Revolution," or Vol. 15 of the published "Documents Relating to the Colonial History of the State of New York," published by Reed, Parsons & Co., Albany, New York, 1887. Also page 261 of "Heitman's Register of Officers of the Continental Army," published by H. B. Heitman, at Washington, D. C.) Captain Thomas Lee's services in the Continental army were equivalent to service in the regular army of to-day.

In regard to my own life, I will say that I was born in Seneca county, New York, October 10th, 1817, and came with my parents to what is now known as Fulton county, Illinois, in 1821. We came down the Ohio river and up the Mississippi and Illinois rivers in a keel boat. The country at that time was a vast wilderness, inhabited only by Indians and abounding with wild animals. It was several years after we came to Illinois before the country became sufficiently settled to establish schools, and I had little opportunity in the years of my youth to obtain an education. What education I did get was obtained at the little log schoolhouses, though in 1836, when I was nineteen years of age, my father sent me to Illinois College, at Jacksonville, Illinois. I had attended college scarcely a year when my father died. He had been engaged in extensive business enterprises, and in consequence of his death I was obliged to leave school and come home and take charge of my mother's business, which put an end to my college life. When I entered Illinois College I took in with me as college chum, William H. Herndon, who for many years was the law partner of Abraham Lincoln, and who was the author of the book entitled "Life of Abraham Lincoln, by W. H. Herndon." I have had something to say of this book in my sketch of the early life of Lincoln.

My father was engaged for many years in farming, and in the mercantile business, and in trading with the Indians, and the early part of my life was spent on the farm, in the store, and in trading with the Indians. I would often take long trips into the country, far away from any white neighbors, in company with Indian traders, whom my father kept employed, and I then learned to speak the Indian language quite well. I at a very early age learned the use of firearms, and was very often out hunting and trapping, as the country in those times abounded in wild game. Great droves of deer and large flocks of wild turkeys could be found everywhere. I have shot wild turkeys when but seven years of age, and have killed deer when twelve years old. I can remember catching eight wolves in steel traps set around the carcass of one dead horse, when I was but twelve years of age. In 1832, when I was fifteen years of age, I carried the mail on horseback, once a week, from Springfield to Monmouth, Illinois, the distance being about 135 miles. I frequently had to swim my horse over streams of water three or four times a day, there being no bridges, with the mailbag strapped across my shoulders to keep the mail from getting wet. I will mention one of my adventures. I was traveling from Monmouth to Knoxville, the distance being twenty miles, and not a house was there between the two villages. A dark and rainy night came on, when I was ten miles from Knoxville, and when I had reached the place where the city of Galesburg now stands the grass was very high in the road, and all of a sudden I heard a hungry pack of wolves set up a tremendous howling right behind my horse, and from the noise they made I supposed that the whole country was alive with wolves, so I applied the whip to my horse, and was not long in getting to Knoxville, and I probably made as good time on horseback as the railroad trains are making at the present time. In the year 1833, when I was sixteen years of age, I took a trip from Havana, in Mason county, Illinois, to what was called the "Lead Mine Country" in the northwestern part of Illinois, a distance of about 225 miles. The greater part of the road ran through an unbroken wilderness. In many places the white settlers were from fifteen to twenty-five miles apart. There were many deep and dangerous streams of water to cross, and it was certainly a long and dangerous trip for a boy to take alone and on horseback. I found many Indians on the road, and sometimes stayed with them over night, and always found them kind and friendly. The cause of my taking the trip at that time was this: My uncle, Joseph Ross, had some three years before gone to the lead mines, taking with him his only child, my cousin Ossian, a boy about five years of age. My uncle was taken sick and died, leaving this boy with strangers, and no one to look after him, and so I went there and brought him home with me. He at the time of this trip was only eight years of age. I was some twenty days in making the trip, and we got home all in good shape. One of the first business enterprises I engaged in after I became of age was to purchase an interest in a steamboat, called the Navigator, which ran from St. Louis, Missouri, to La Salle on the Illinois river. I held the position on her of steamboat clerk. After running on her for a year, I sold out my interest, and then took a wife. I was married on the 1st day of January, 1840, to Jane R. Kirkpatrick at Canton, Illinois. Upon our marriage we went to Havana, Illinois, and there kept the Havana Hotel, and also the ferry across the Illinois river, and we engaged in farming and stockraising. I was later appointed postmaster at Havana, Illinois, by President Martin Van Buren. In 1844 I removed to and settled on a farm of forty acres adjoining the town of Vermont in Fulton county, Illinois, and as I had never learned a trade, nor studied for any profession, I had to rely on my hands and head for a living in the world. I settled down on my little farm and went to work, and planted out a fine orchard, which in after years yielded me from eight to ten thousand bushels of fruit a year. I added to my little farm from time to time, until I had a farm of 400 acres, all well improved. I also engaged in buying lands and improving them, and selling them to such emigrants as came to the country and wished to purchase improved farms. I continued in that business until I had became the purchaser and had disposed of six farms in Fulton county and fourteen farms in McDonough county, Illinois, and those farms are at the present time among the very best in those two counties. I have good reason to believe that I have had a greater number of acres of land broken up and put in cultivation than any other man that has ever lived in McDonough county. I only mention these facts to show that I have not been an idler or drone in the great hive of human progress, but have taken some part in helping to develop the great resources of the country.

My principal occupation through life has been that of a farmer, although I engaged in the mercantile business in connection with my farming operations for about ten years. I have never been an office seeker, and have had but little desire to hold office, although I have held a few small offices. I have held the office of town councilman, town treasurer, supervisor, justice of the peace and postmaster. I was twice elected treasurer and director of a railroad. I have usually voted the Democratic ticket, but when I came to California, in 1881, I attended the Democratic State Convention, and found that a large majority of the delegates to the convention were saloonkeepers and wholesale liquor dealers, and that the prominent questions which came before the convention were the repeal of the Sunday law, which was then the law of the state of California, and the enactment of laws in the interests of liquor dealers, so I left the Democratic party and joined the Prohibition party. And at the State Prohibition Convention, in 1884, I was selected as a delegate to the National Prohibition Convention that was held in the city of Pittsburgh in 1884, at which convention the Hon. John P. St. John was nominated for president. At that convention twenty-eight states and three territories were represented by 465 delegates. It was at this convention that I first had the opportunity and the pleasure of seeing and hearing that grand and noble lady, Miss Frances E. Willard. She placed in nomination for president John P. St. John, and on that occasion she made one of the most eloquent and powerful speeches that was heard during the convention. I felt a little honored in being chosen with her on the committee that drafted the platform and resolutions which were unanimously adopted by the convention. I have been a member of some temperance organization for over half a century. I have never indulged in the use of liquor nor tobacco in any form, and during the more than eighty years of my life I do not think that I ever had to exceed more than five days of sickness, and I attribute my good health and length of years very materially to abstaining from the use of liquor and tobacco. My wife and I lived together lacking but three days of fifty-eight years. There were born to us six children, four sons and two daughters. Our first child, Ossian, died when eighteen months old. All my other children are married and have families. They are Harriet S. Hall, Frank W. Ross, Mary F. Childs, George C. Ross and Joseph L. Ross. I have twelve grandchildren and four great-grandchildren. I have been a member of the Presbyterian church for sixty years. I was converted under the preaching of the Rev. Dr. David Nelson, at a Presbyterian campmeeting held near the town of Canton, Illinois, in 1838. I first joined the Presbyterian church, at Canton, Illinois, in 1838. I have been a member of the Presbyterian church at Vermont, Illinois, and also of the Presbyterian church at Macomb, Illinois. I held the office of presiding elder in each of those churches, and have represented each of them in presbytery. I am at the present time a member of the First Presbyterian church of Oakland, California, which has a membership of over thirteen hundred.

The End.

www.ingramcontent.com/pod-product-compliance
Lightning Source LLC
Chambersburg PA
CBHW031817220426
43662CB00007B/683